W9-DJE-512

# SOMETHING FROM NOTHING

CHARTWELL
BOOKS INC.

**AUTHOR:** Eve Harlow

**EDITOR:** Angela Jeffs

**ART EDITOR:** Stewart Cowley

PHOTOGRAPHERS
John Gill: pages 70, 76, 77, 84, 85, 90, 96
Chris Lewis: 15, 16, 19, 20, 22, 23, 24, 28, 32,
66, 67, 68, 69, 74, 80, 81, 82, 83, 86, 87, 88,
89, 93 Neil Lorimer: 94 Alan Meek: 6, 8, 9, 10,
11

DESIGNERS
Veronica Burns: designs 49 Kate Cooper: 24,
40, 41, 55, 90 Peter Cottam: 14, 17, 20, 45,
62, 66, 69, 81, 84, 89, 93 Katie Dyson: 32
Anna Griffiths: 33, 34, 35 Eve Harlow: 5, 15,
16, 18, 19, 21, 22, 25, 26, 27, 28, 29, 31, 36,
37, 50, 51, 54, 56, 57, 58, 61, 64, 70, 71, 72,
73, 74, 75, 76, 77, 78, 79, 80, 82, 83, 85, 86,
87, 88, 91, 92, 94, 95, 96, 98, 99, 100, 101
Audrey Hersch: 46, 52 Alan Meek: 1, 2, 3, 4, 6,
7, 8, 9, 10, 11

CREDITS
Camera Press Fur Sie: pages 12, 21, 26, 29,
30, 72, 73, 78, 79, 92 Tee Itse: 14, 18
Paf International 31

All Illustrations by Barbara Firth

*Published in the United States by*
*Chartwell Books Inc., A Division*
*of Book Sales Inc., 110 Enterprise*
*Avenue, Secaucus, New Jersey 07094*

© *Copyright Marshall Cavendish Limited 1973, 1977*

*First printing 1973*
*Second printing 1977*

*Printed in Hong Kong*

*ISBN 0 89009 151 X*

## About this book . .

Parents today have almost forgotten that when they were young they made a great many of their toys and amusements from what adults considered to be rubbish. Greengrocers were begged for two wooden boxes and enterprising boys knocked together a racing go-cart in the space of a morning. Girls collected pretty buttons, bits of glass and small bottles and arranged 'grottoes'– small collections of treasures. And wasn't it all great fun? Every tin can, wooden and cardboard box and scrap of coloured paper could be turned into something useful.

It wasn't that children were cleverer then, and nor is it necessarily a skill that they have lost in the affluent society. Parents seemed to have more time and passed on ideas and games which they in turn had learned from *their* parents. Most of the things in this book have been made by parents and a great many of the ideas were gleaned from grandparents and updated to modern materials. Some of the toys can be made by children themselves while others need adult expertise and will make gifts for children.

Once you begin to make some of the things, other ideas for toys and models will occur to you and be remembered. Keeping the old children's games and toys alive in our memory is part of the fun of being a parent and through this book, you can pass on to your children the joy and satisfaction that comes from making everything to play with yourself, from almost nothing at all.

# CONTENTS

1

*Simple peg-board panels hinged to make a grocer's shop*

# 5

Learn to play tip-e-tee – it's a game of skill !

# 2

(Left) Make these colourful baby bricks from wood offcuts

# 6

Surprise, surprise – it's a Jack-in-the-box

# 3

(Above) Versatile box-train unit for nursery rides, toy storage or a shop counter

# 7

Paddle boat for bath-time mariners

# 4

An all-wood sailing boat with cotton sail and swing boom

# 8

Push-along toy that always keeps it's balance

9

# 9

(Left and below) Get going on this fast-moving tyre traveller

# 10

(Far left) Score a bull's eye with these giant-sized lawn darts

# 11

Walk tall on height-adjustable stilts

Next week – East Lynne ! An old-time
theatre to make from a cardboard box

## 13

*(Below) No hang-up problems with this happy rhino*

## 14

*(Right) Build houses, castles, shops and stores from small boxes, paper and paint*

**23**
*Lanky child-sized puppet to make in cardboard or wood*

# 24

Fairy tale character dolls to illustrate a
favourite story

## 25

(Above) Four pompon toys – a hedgehog, snake, chick and ladybird

## 26

A wicked witch puppet from cotton reels

## 27

Put this racer on the floor and watch it go !

## 28
Learn to knit the easy way with this knitting Nancy

## 29
Popgun to shoot paper pellets across the room

## 30
(Top right) Soft play balls to make in patchwork pentagons and segments

# 31

*(Left) Let's play Indians in a bed-sheet wigwam*

# 32

*(Above) Practical and pretty to keep sleeping dolls tidy*

25

**38**

*Tomorrow's heirlooms to make in patchwork*

**39**

*Cherry-laden trees for a standing forest*

# 40

*(Far left) Oh to be as tall as a giraffe and a half. A measuring wall hanging to stick and sew*

# 41

*(Left) Exquisitely-detailed Victorian doll's house*

# 42

*(Below) Lots of ideas for sparkling Christmas trees*

**43**

*(Left) A girl's best friend is likely to be this giant rag doll*

**44**

*(Above) A place for everything and everything in its place*

*Mrs Tabitha Twitchet is at home – the
light's on in this nursery lamp*

# Instructions for designs 1·45

## Tools and Equipment

Apart from the tools listed in the wooden toys section, very little equipment is needed for making the things in this book.

You'll find that you'll improvize with things that are already around the house for most of the makes, but for almost every toy you need a sharp knife. Craft shops and do-it-yourself shops sell a short handled, stubby knife with removable blades which is ideal for most cutting jobs – and the knife will have a wide use in the household apart from toymaking.

A strong pair of paper cutting scissors would be useful, and a small, sharp, pointed pair for intricate cutting out.

A good paint brush is an investment both in time and good finish and one with an inch wide head would be sufficient for most of the paint jobs in this book.

Note: Always check that the paints you use ARE SAFE! They should be both lead free and flame proof.

## Adhesives

All through this book, references are made to adhesives of different kinds. The right kind of adhesive for the job not only makes toymaking easier but gives the finished toy a longer life.

**Fabric adhesive** is a latex-based substance, usually white coloured. Copydex is one of the best known.

**Rubber solution** is usually recommended for paper and light card and is best where paper has to be mounted onto card. Rubber solution does not stain and can be cleaned off a surface with a finger tip.

**All-purpose adhesives** This term is used for adhesives which are designated on the container as being suitable for paper, card, plastic, wood, ceramics etc. Uhu and Bostik fall into this category.

**Contact or impact adhesives** These adhesives do what the name implies – bond on contact.

**Water-soluble pastes** These are available in jars or plastic bottle applicators and are recommended for pasting tissue paper and similar papers together.

**Woodworker's adhesive** has been used for constructing the wooden toys.

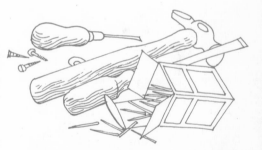

## Making wooden toys

In this chapter, only very simple tools have been used. Complicated wood joints have been avoided but a really good woodworker's adhesive is recommended. The tools used to make the toys in this section are:

Handsaw
Tennon saw
Fretsaw
Hacksaw
Small hammer
Surform 'plane'
Square
Hand drill
Screwdriver
Small vice

# Grocery shop

**A simple shop made of three pegboard panels fitted with drop-in hinges, so that the panels can be taken apart for storage. Shelves are fitted on metal peg board fittings.**

Materials you will need:
3 pieces of pegboard each 3 ft square
2 inch by 1 inch battening
4 drop-in hinges or loose-pin hinges
Panel pins
¼ inch plywood
Woodworker's adhesive

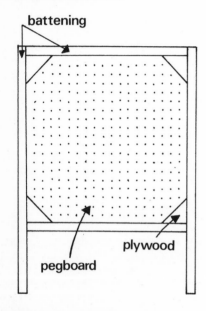

**To make one panel**
Cut two pieces of battening, each 4 ft long and glue them on opposite edges of the pegboard, ranging the top edges.
Pin the battening, working from the top edges.
Cut two more pieces of battening, 2 ft 8 inches wide for the cross-members. Glue and pin these to the pegboard in the same way.
Cut four right-angled triangles of plywood. Pin and glue one into each corner These will provide strength and rigidity.
Make three panels in the same way.
Fix the drop-in hinges to the edges of the panels.
The left hand panel is fitted with the 'female' part of the hinges on the right hand edge. The centre panel has four 'male' parts, two on each side and the right hand panel has two 'female'

fittings, fixed to the left hand side. The top hinges should be fixed about 3 inches from the top of the panels and the lower level with the bottom edge of the pegboard.
Make as many shelves as required from 6 inch by ½ inch wood, attached to the pegboard with pegboard fittings.

# Off-cuts brick set

Use the shapes of wood off-cuts as they are but make sure that the faces are square and absolutely smooth.
Round off the edges slightly with sand paper. Paint in bright colours with enamel or cover with two coats of clear varnish.

# Box train

**A single box unit makes a good push-along toy for a young child, or, on its side, acts as a counter for the grocer's shop. Make three boxes and paint them different colours. Screw a hook at one end and a ring at the other end on each box and link the boxes to make a nursery train.**

Materials you will need:
1 piece of blockboard 16 inches wide by 24 inches for the base
2 pieces of ¼ inch plywood 11½ inches deep and 24 inches wide for the sides
2 pieces of ¼ inch plywood 11½ inches deep and 15 inches wide for the ends
2 16 inch lengths of 3 inch by ½ inch moulding
4 triangular shaped pieces of plywood
Panel pins

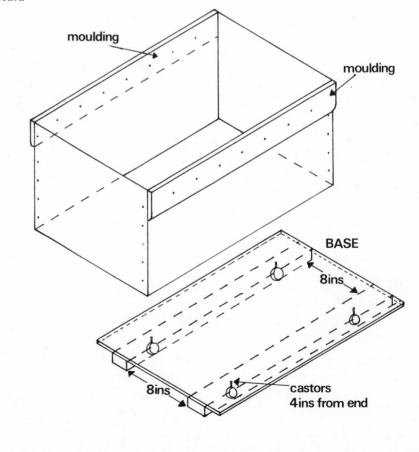

**3.** *The simple construction of the box train unit: the moulding is pinned to the end pieces and the four castors screw into the two bracing supports under the base board*

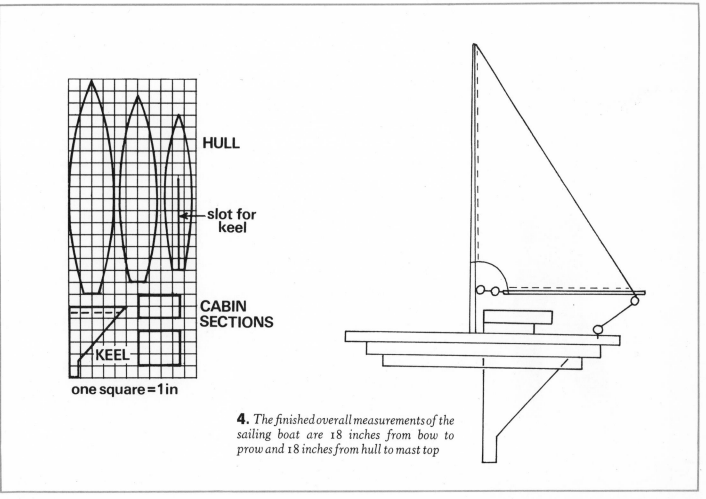

**HULL**

**slot for keel**

**CABIN SECTIONS**

**KEEL**

one square = 1 in

**4.** *The finished overall measurements of the sailing boat are 18 inches from bow to prow and 18 inches from hull to mast top*

---

¾ inch nails
4 castors
2 24 inch lengths of 2 inch by 1 inch wood
Woodworker's adhesive

Glue and pin the moulding to the top edge of the two side pieces.
Glue and pin the four sides of the box together.
On the underside of the blockboard base section, glue and pin the two lengths of 2 inch by 1 inch wood, 8 inches apart. Screw in the castors, 4 inches from the ends.
Glue and nail the base to the box.
Strengthen corners with triangular shaped pieces of plywood.
Paint with enamel.

**Putting in a seat**
If a seat is required in the box, cut a piece of blockboard 16 inches by 12 inches. Cut three pieces of 2 inch by 2 inch, each 12 inches long. Screw these to the inside of the box, 3 inches from the base board, to form supports for the seat. Screw the seat in position.

4

# Sailing boat

**Here is a wooden sailing boat which would make a good father-and-son project although mother's help may be needed with the fabric sail.**

Materials you will need:
½ inch pinewood for the hull sections
Formica or similar material for the keel
Lead solder
18 inches ⅜ inch dowelling
4 screw eyes
Twine
Cotton fabric for a sail
Woodworker's adhesive
Epoxy adhesive
Enamel paints or clear varnish

Draw a pattern and cut out the three hull sections, the Formica keel and the two cabin sections. Saw a slot for the keel in the shortest length of hull sec-tion as shown in the diagram. Glue the three hull sections together. Glue the cabin sections together and glue the cabin to the hull immediately over where the keel section will be. Fix the lead solder to the keel with Epoxy. Slip the keel into the slot and also fix with Epoxy adhesive.

**Making the sail**
Cut the dowelling into two pieces, one 10 inches long and the other 18 inches long.
Cut a triangle of fabric 19 inches on the vertical side and 11 inches on the horizontal side. Make a narrow hem on the third side. Make a casing to take the dowelling on the 19 inch and 11 inch sides. Slip the dowelling rods through. Insert screw eyes and tie these together with twine to join the mast and boom. Drill a hole in the deck just in front of the cabin section and insert the mast. Insert a screw eye to the end of the boom and another to the deck.
Tie the free end of the boom to the deck.

# Jack-in-the-box

**The origins of Jack-in-the-box toys are obscure but it may once have been a reproduction of the sudden appearance of the Devil or of an imp. However, Jacks are still firm favourites with children and this one is made using the head from a broken doll.**

Materials you will need:
Head from a broken doll (or make one from papier mâché)
3 pieces of hardboard 6 inches square
2 pieces of hardboard $5\frac{7}{8}$ inches by 6 inches deep
Lengths of $\frac{1}{2}$ inch by $\frac{1}{2}$ inch wood
Fabric adhesive tape, 1 inch wide
3 hair roller springs
Panel pins
Cardboard
Flat hook and screw eye
Staples
Fabric for dress and scraps of felt

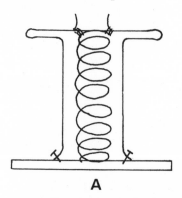

**A**

▲ *Showing how to fix the spring*

▼ *The construction of the box*

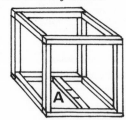

Construct the box first. The finished dimensions are 6 inches by 6 inches by 6 inches. Cut lengths of wood for the struts and glue and pin the struts in position. Do not fix the hardboard sides on at this stage. Cut a strut 5 inches long and glue this along the centre of the piece of hardboard which will be the base (one of the 6 inch square pieces). The Jack doll will be fixed to this strut.

Make the lid of the box from cardboard. Cut a 6 inch square and glue a small piece of wood on the front edge. Screw an eye fastening into the wood. Remove the coverings from the hair rollers. Join them together end to end with soft wire. Open up the springs slightly to strengthen them. Trim off rings of spring if necessary. Fix the bottom of the spring to the strut with staples.

**Jack's dress**
Cut a dress shape from the fabric approximately 12 inches deep and 7 inches wide from wrist to wrist.
Cut the arms in one with the main body of the dress. Cut four little hand shapes from the felt. Make up two shapes for each hand, stuffing a little cotton wool between the pieces. Stitch the hands to the ends of the sleeves. Make the dress up on the wrong side leaving the neck edge and the hem open. Stitch and glue the dress neck round the neck of the doll's head. Slip the dress over the spring and pin the hem to the strut.
Stitch through the dress at the shoulders to the spring to keep the head balanced. Now assemble the sides of the box, noting that the two larger, square shapes go opposite each other. Glue and pin the box sides.
Attach the lid with fabric tape and secure with two or three panel pins. Drop the base of the box into position from outside the box and glue and pin in position. Cover the box with gift wrapping paper and fix the hook to the front to correspond with the screw eye.

# Tip-e-tee

Tip-e-tee is a very old game, played in many parts of the world and known by a variety of names. Tip-e-tee is the name the game was known by in 19th century East London.
Country boys used to cut sturdy beech twigs and whittle the ends to make their tip-e-tees; to make a good-looking toy, use 1 inch by 1 inch hardwood and cut a piece 6 inches long. Whittle the ends to a blunt point. Paint with stripes or patterns if desired.
To play tip-e-tee, rest it on a stone, a brick or a low wall with one pointed end protruding slightly. Take a piece of wood or a bat in the hand and bring it down on the tip-e-tee end smartly. The tip-e-tee will jump in the air and the skill lies in managing to hit it hard and away while still in the air. As the player becomes more proficient, the tip-e-tee can be hit up from the ground itself. Warn children to stand well clear of a tip-e-tee player, while he makes his hit.

# Paddle boat

**This neat little paddle boat is so simple in construction that a boy could probably make it for himself. The paddle is powered by a rubber band which fits into the notched stern. Wind up the 'motor' by turning the paddle with a finger.**

Materials you will need:
$\frac{1}{2}$ inch wood
2 pieces of Formica or similar

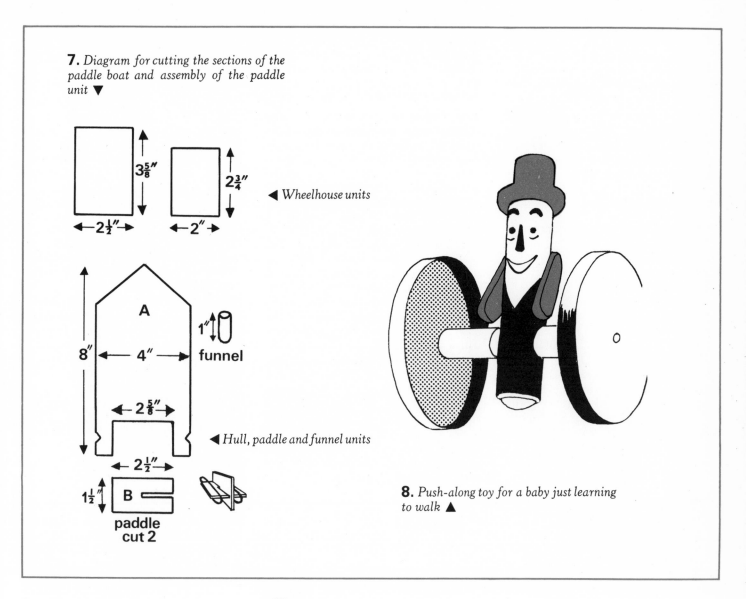

**7.** *Diagram for cutting the sections of the paddle boat and assembly of the paddle unit* ▼

3⅝″

2⅜″

◄ *Wheelhouse units*

2½″

2″

A

8″

4″

1″

funnel

2⅝″

◄ *Hull, paddle and funnel units*

2½″

1½″

B

paddle
cut 2

**8.** *Push-along toy for a baby just learning to walk* ▲

material 2½ inches by 1½ inches
2 elastic bands
2 washers
1 inch of ½ inch dowelling

Cut the hull and wheel-house units from the diagram. The dowelling makes a funnel. Notches are cut at one end of the stern and a section is cut away to take the paddle unit.
Cut two pieces of laminate as shown in diagram B and slot them together, glueing with adhesive.
Fit a rubber band over two of the fins. Slip a washer over the two rubber band loops at each end.
Position the paddle wheel and loop the rubber bands over the notches.
Varnish the vessel or paint with enamel.

# Push-along toy

**The weight glued on the base of the push-along toy keeps the little man standing upright all the time. Cut the arms from an easily worked wood such as balsa or make them from stiff cardboard.**

Materials you will need:
2 wheels (lids from paint cans can be used but the wheels on the push-along illustrated were hub caps from an old, small car.)
5 inches ¾ inch dowelling
4 inch nail with the head removed
8 inches of broomstick
A fishing weight
1 inch nails
Wood adhesive

Epoxy adhesive

Pierce the 'wheels' ready to accept the nail.
Cut the dowelling in half. Drill a hole at one end of both pieces, about ½ inch deep. Glue the nail into one piece of dowelling with epoxy adhesive. Drill a hole through the piece of broomstick about 1 inch from one end.
Make a pair of wooden arms and paint the broomstick to look like a little man. Pin the arms on with nails.
Glue the fishing weight to the bottom of the broomstick figure. Push the figure onto the nail which is glued into dowelling. Glue the other end of the nail into the second piece of dowelling. Nail the wheels to the ends of the dowelling.

# Tyre traveller

Here is a different kind of wheeled toy to make and one that costs very little in materials. It's safe for children aged from about seven years and fun for both boys and girls.

Materials you will need:
An old tyre
Block board larger than the dimensions of the tyre
Half round moulding
4 large sized castors
Screws, nuts and bolts

Cut the block board about 3 inches larger all round than the tyre.
Glue and pin half round moulding to the edges.
Fix the tyre onto the block board with two nuts and bolts, fixing them inside the tyre and placing them on opposite sides of the tyre from each other.
Screw castors underneath the block board, one at each corner.
Give the tyre a coat of paint for good looks.

# Lawn darts

Lawn darts is a game of skill and should only be played by older children under adult supervision.

Materials you will need:
3 12 inch lengths of 1 inch dowelling
3 6 inch nails with the heads cut off
Pieces of laminated plastic for fins

Drill a hole in one end of the dowelling to receive the cut end of the nail. Leave the point protruding about 3 inches. Glue the nail into the dowelling. Cut two fins from the laminated plastic to the size and shape given in the diagram. Cut one in half. Make cuts with a saw in the top end of the dowelling to the depth of the fin in a cross. Insert the whole fin in one cut and glue. Insert the half fins in the remaining cuts and glue. Paint with coloured enamels.
Make a target for lawn darts from a circle of paper cut to a diameter of 36 inches. Paint score circles with poster paints and aim for a bull's eye.

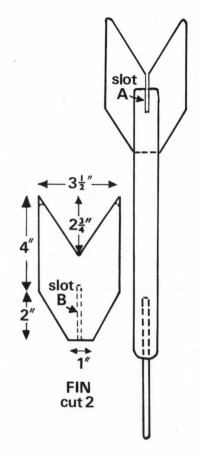

▲ *Cut two fins and cut one in half*

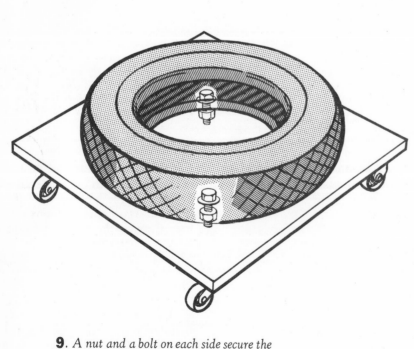

**9**. *A nut and a bolt on each side secure the tyre to the blockboard base* ▲

**10**. *Stand at least ten paces from the target to play lawn darts* ▼

# 11

# Stilts

**Stilts are for children aged nine years and upwards. Make them with adjustable steps because these help while the child is learning to walk on them.**

Materials you will need:
2 lengths of wood $1\frac{3}{4}$ inches by $1\frac{1}{2}$ inches for stilts
12 inches of 3 inch by $1\frac{1}{2}$ inch wood for steps
4 pieces of threaded studding 4 inches long
4 wing nuts
Sandpaper
Enamel or varnish

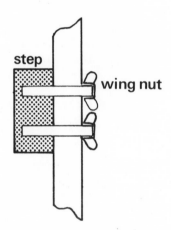

▲ *Step bolted to the stilt with wing nut and threaded studding*

Stilts should be cut to a length to suit the child. The pair illustrated are 5 ft 3 inches long and are the right size for a 10 year old.

Choose $1\frac{3}{4}$ inch by $1\frac{1}{2}$ softwood. Plane down one end for about 12 inches to make a round handle.

Cut two 5-6 inch deep steps from 3 inch by $1\frac{1}{2}$ inch wood and bolt them to the stilt with threaded studding. To do this, drill two holes through the stilt and to correspond, through the wooden step. Two lengths of threaded studding are inserted and glued into position in the step. Wing nuts secure the step to the stilt. Holes could be drilled in each stilt at varying heights so that the steps can be lowered or raised for children of different ages.

Smooth the stilts off with sandpaper and either paint or finish with two coats of varnish.

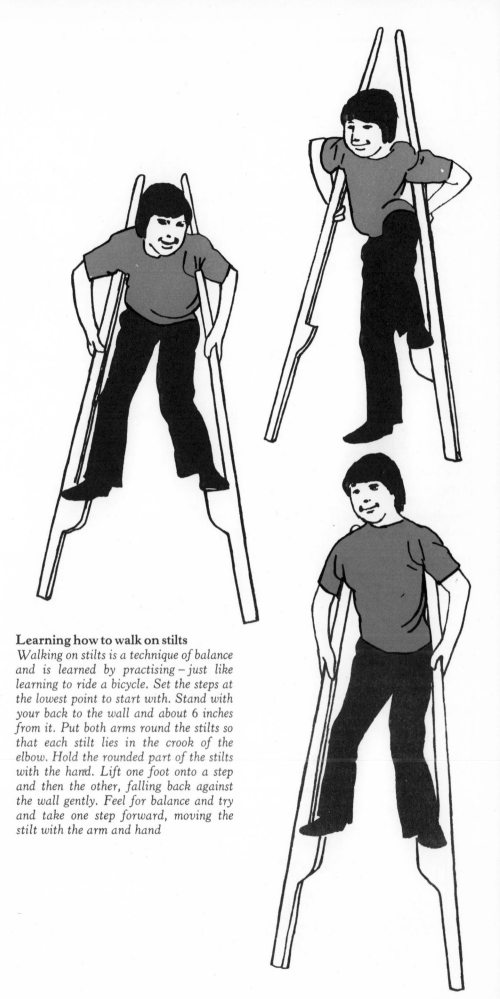

### Learning how to walk on stilts

*Walking on stilts is a technique of balance and is learned by practising – just like learning to ride a bicycle. Set the steps at the lowest point to start with. Stand with your back to the wall and about 6 inches from it. Put both arms round the stilts so that each stilt lies in the crook of the elbow. Hold the rounded part of the stilts with the hand. Lift one foot onto a step and then the other, falling back against the wall gently. Feel for balance and try and take one step forward, moving the stilt with the arm and hand*

**glue tab into slit in wood strip**

**one square=1in**

**12**. *Use these characters life size or reduce them to fit your theatre* ▲

▼ *If a picture frame isn't available, cut a frame from card*

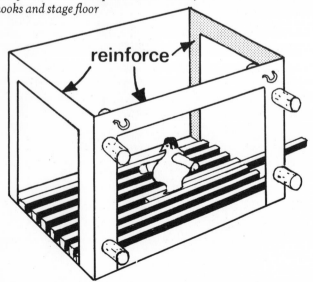

▼*Reinforced box complete with corks, hooks and stage floor*

**reinforce**

# Toy theatre

**A charming toy theatre in 19th century style made from a large cardboard or wooden box.
Write your own script for a play and make jointed characters from plywood, hardboard or cardboard.**

Materials you need:
Cardboard or wooden box of any size
Picture frame to fit the long side of the box or cut a frame from laminated cardboard
Lengths of ½ inch by ½ inch wood strip
Plywood, cardboard or hardboard for cut-out characters
Small screws
2 small cup hooks
½ inch dowelling for supporting the curtain
Small curtain rings for the curtain
Fabric for curtain
6 corks
Strong all-purpose adhesive
Covering paper
Paper, felt, card for scenery

Seal the box flaps with adhesive. Cut a hole in one long side for the theatre front. Leave a margin of cardboard all round of about 2½ inches.
Cut a hole in both short sides for the wings. Strengthen the stage front section with 2½ inch wide strips of card. The stage front has to take the weight of the curtains etc., and needs the rigidity. Glue the strips of card firmly .Glue two corks on the inside of the box behind the upper stage front. These are for inserting the cup hooks. Screw the hooks in and leave the corks to dry out.
Glue four corks to the stage front in the positions shown on the drawing. These are to hold the frame clear of the curtain unit.

## To make the stage

Cut lengths of ½ inch by ½ inch wood strip to exactly fit the width of the stage area. Glue the strips to the bottom of the box exactly ½ inch apart and parallel to each other. Paint the sticks and stage bottom white. Cut more lengths of wood strip to about three-quarters of the width of the stage. The characters are glued into the end of these strips.
To manipulate the players, slide the sticks between the sticks making the stage.
Make the curtains of a light-weight fabric. Stitch the tops of the curtains to

rings and slip them onto a length of dowelling. Hook the dowelling onto the cup hooks.

## Frame front

An old picture frame can be glued and pinned to the corks for a charming stage front. If a picture frame isn't available, cut a cardboard frame and cover it with a rich coloured velvet fabric.

## Character figures

Design and cut these from plywood or hardboard with a fretsaw or cut them from stiff cardboard. The arms and legs are jointed and attached with small screws or, if cardboard is being used, use brass paper clips. Paint and decorate the characters—and on with the play!

# Animal hanger

If anything will make them hang their coats up it's this smiling rhino. Cut the rhino head from plywood and paint it with enamel. Fix it to a piece of ½ inch wood using a through housing joint.
The graph diagram indicates a scale of 1 square to 1 inch, giving a finished rhino head of 15 inches deep by 12 inches wide.
To make a smaller head, adapt the pattern by taking 1 square of the pattern to represent ½ inch.
Fix the rhino head to a door or to the wall by driving screws through the corners of the ½ inch thick wood mount.

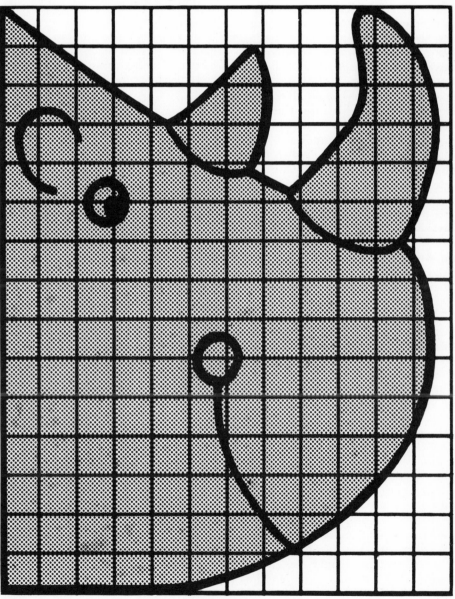

**13**. *To make a rhino head 15 inches deep, use the pattern to a scale of 1 sq = 1 inch* ▲

# Paper and card

The average family has access to a wide variety of types of cardboard which can be utilized to make toys and models. Grocery stores are usually pleased to dispose of cartons and boxes and many of these are strongly built and of a good size. The side panels of egg boxes made of laminated card have been used for many of the toys in this book. Shops selling electrical equipment and similar merchandise are a source of really thick cardboard, and food boxes (such as those containing cereals) are good because the card is flexible and the backs and fronts of boxes will provide good sized pieces. Paper should be carefully hoarded – keep gift wrapping papers, the paper bags from shops which are printed with an all-over pattern, and brown paper. If only brown paper is available to you, print your own all-over designs on it using coloured inks or paints and using tools from the kitchen as printing 'plates'. Fork tins, pastry cutters, the potato masher, bottle bases, corks and bottle caps are just a few of the things with interesting shape possibilities.

Coloured paper, available in sheets of different sizes from art shops and stationers, has been used on some of the toys in this section. Although these papers are comparatively inexpensive to buy, they aren't necessary to the effectiveness of the toy and one can economise by looking elsewhere for coloured paper. Glossy magazines sometimes feature large spreads of colour pictures and areas of these, judiciously cut away, can provide interesting and exciting colour effects. The detail of the photograph is lost entirely when the picture is cut up in this way and looks rather like an abstract design. If a large area is to be covered, build up a montage of scraps, matching colours and tones wherever possible.

The average household usually has an enormous amount of paper coming in the form of packaging and containers and some of it is superbly designed.

# 14
## Model village

The model village illustrated was made from a variety of small boxes, some food boxes, a toothpaste carton, a small box which had contained aspirin and others. Collect boxes until you have a good selection to work with.

To begin, pile the boxes together, one on another until the shapes of houses begin to form. Glue the boxes together and cover with scraps of coloured paper. Cut windows and doors separately rather than drawing them on, because the finished effect is prettier.

From bigger food boxes, cut strips for walls and gardens, covering them with coloured paper or felt.

Small details like chimney pots can be made from small pieces of thin card, rolled into tubes and glued.

Round shapes for towers can either be cut from canisters which have held herbs or spices, or can be cut from cardboard and taped into tube shapes.

# 15
## Gyroscope Game

This game is made with the lid of a box and a piece of card. A gyroscope spinner will work for most table games when the die can't be found. Trace the pattern of the hexagon shape onto a piece of white paper. Colour and number the six segments. Cut the paper out and paste it onto a piece of card. Cut the shape out with a sharp knife. Push a cocktail stick through the middle.

To use the spinner in place of a die, spin the shape and when it settles on one of its six sides, that is the score.

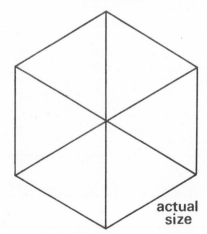

**actual size**

## Two-in-one-box-game

The box lid illustrated measures $9\frac{1}{2}$ inches by $11\frac{1}{2}$ inches but any size of box or lid would do.

Cover the outside of the box with gift paper.

Cut two corks in half and glue one half inside the lid in each of the corners.

Cut a piece of card to fit into the box exactly. Cut small holes in it at one end. Triangles were cut in the box illustrated because they are easy to shape with a knife. Cut one of the holes larger than the others and position it in the centre of the group of holes. Cover the piece of card with brightly coloured paper.

On the wrong side, cut the paper through the holes.

On the right side, push the paper through with the finger tip.

Mark the biggest hole 'penalty' and number the remaining holes for scoring. Fit the card into the box resting on the corks.

Spin the spinner and to score, the point of the spinner must settle into one of the holes. If the spinner doesn't go into a hole then there is no score. If the spinner goes into the penalty hole, all the previous scores are lost, and the player must begin again.

## Colour match game

Trace off the hexagon shape from the diagram and extend the arms until you have a shape 4 inches in diameter.

Trace the shape onto white paper. Colour each of the sections. Paste the hexagon down into the box lid. Spin the spinner and the player wins when the spinner settles on the hexagon with its colour segment down on a matching colour.

To develop the game, each player tries for all the colours, one after another until all six have been scored.

# 16
## Collection displays

Children love to have somewhere to display their collections of stones, shells and other treasures. Six animal food cans glued together into a pyramid and painted make an ideal shelf display unit or, line a wooden fruit box with card and then felt, and hang it on the wall for a miniature pin board.

An old picture frame, nailed to the front of a wooden box makes an unusual yet effective display cabinet—cardboard shelving and dividers are added.

The wall unit illustrated is constructed from a cardboard box with holes cut in the base. Each hole is cut to fit a food box. The food boxes were cut down to two inches deep to give a uniform appearance and the boxes are held in position in the holes with tape at the back. Choose food boxes of different shapes or cut one side away from tube-shaped cartons. Paint the insides of the boxes black or white to display things to their best advantage. Paint the outside of each with a bright coloured poster paint. Cover the main box with gay wrapping paper.

To achieve a good finish, cover what is to be the front of the display unit with a single sheet of paper after the holes have been cut. From the wrong side, cut the paper through the holes in a cross, taking the cuts right into the corners. Lift the cut edges through the holes and glue the edges down on the inside of the box.

The display box can either be stood on a shelf or, if it is to be hung, push a length of dowelling through the top corners and tie twine to it.

# 17
# Tell-the-time-clock

A delightful clock face to make from cardboard and coloured papers to help a child to learn to tell the time. You might place transfers of favourite animals at the three, six, nine and 12 numerals to help him to remember quarter past, half past, quarter to and the hour. The clock can be made from felt instead of paper if desired, with pretty flower motifs round the edges.

Materials you will need:
Stiff cardboard
6 inches ribbon
Coloured paper
Nut, bolt and washers
Strong adhesive
1 inch curtain ring
Rub-down numerals
Sharp knife

Cut two squares of cardboard 12 inches by 12 inches. Fold the ribbon and pass it through the curtain ring. Glue the ribbon ends onto one corner of one piece of card, so that the card hangs as a diamond shape. Glue the second piece of card onto the back.

▼ *Diagram for two clock hands showing position for bolt placing*

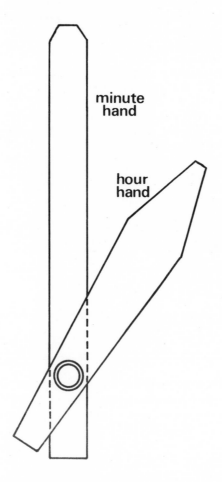

minute hand

hour hand

Find the exact centre and make a hole large enough for the bolt to fit.

Cover the face of the card with coloured paper. Cut a circle of white paper 10 inches diameter for the clock face. Glue it to the front. Using a protractor, divide the edge of the circle into 30° segments so that the numerals are properly spaced. Mark the points and put down the numerals. Cut a star shape for the centre of the clock face and glue over the hole, then cut the hole again. Cut two hands the same size as the diagram painting one black and one red.

Fit the hands to the clock face, with the bolt, placing washers at both sides of each hand. Screw the nut onto the bolt at the back.

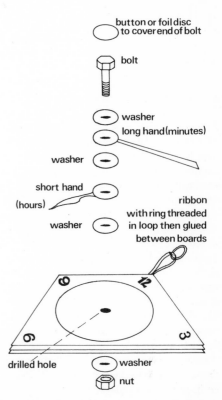

button or foil disc to cover end of bolt

bolt

washer
long hand (minutes)

washer

short hand
(hours)

washer

ribbon with ring threaded in loop then glued between boards

drilled hole    washer

nut

▲ *Mounting the hands onto the clock face*

# 18
# Roll 'em

A very simple marble game to make from a piece of cardboard or a box. Cut the cardboard to shape as shown in the diagram. Score along the fold on the wrong side with the back of a knife blade. Stick tape along the fold on the scored side. Cut out five holes along the edge of the middle panel. Paint the Roll 'em to look like a fairground booth. Number the holes and add the word 'Roll 'em' using rub-down letters and numerals— or cut the characters from a magazine. Roll marbles into the holes to score.

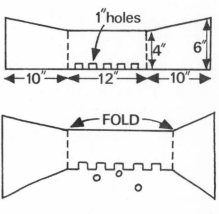

1" holes

4"    6"

←10"→ ←12"→ ←10"→

←FOLD→

43

# 19
## Boomerang

This boomerang will work equally well made from cardboard or paper. The size is unimportant—you can make it as small as three inches across or as large as 12 inches using the diagram as a basis. Cut a true right angled shape, about 1½ inches wide across the arms. Round off the ends of the arms.

Hold the arms of the boomerang with the angle towards your body and give the boomerang a bias by twisting it slightly.

Balance the boomerang on the edge of a table or on the edge of a book held in the left hand. One arm should protrude over the edge with the angle towards you. Hit the arm sharply with the right hand or a pencil. The boomerang will swing away in an arc—and should return!

Trace the shape in the diagram below for a 4 inch boomerang. For a larger toy, draw up a pattern first.

▼ *Graph of the boomerang*

# 20
## Kaleidoscope

**The word kaleidoscope is derived from two Greek words, 'kalos' meaning beautiful and 'eidos' meaning form. The wonderful patterns produced within this remarkable toy are beautiful and you can make a kaleidoscope using simple materials around your home. The one illustrated is 8 inches tall and 2¼ inches in diameter.**

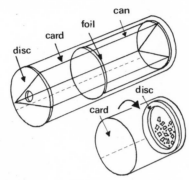

▲*Construction of the kaleidoscope*

Materials you will need to make a kaleidoscope on a 2¼ inch diameter can:
A tall slim can
Piece of foil from a foil baking tin
Cardboard, medium and thick
Cellophane
Grease proof paper
Sweet wrappings (Cellophane, tin foil etc.)
Adhesive

Cut the can open at both ends. Cut a piece of foil 7¼ inches deep by 4 inches wide. (This is deeper than the can). Fold the foil lengthwise down the middle. Open it to a right-angled 'V' and slide it into the can. It should fit in width. Glue it to the can at the edges.

Cut a piece of card 7¾ inches deep by 7⅝ inches. Wrap it round the can and the protruding foil. Sellotape the edges with a flush join.

Cut a disc of card 2¼ inches in diameter with a hole in the middle about the diameter of a pencil. Glue the disc to the cardboard tube at the foil end. Cover with a gift wrapping paper, both to hold the disc firmly and to give the tube an attractive finish.

Onto this tube slips a shorter tube containing the kaleidoscope 'scraps'. Make this part as follows:

Stand the kaleidoscope on a small piece of thick card (at least ⅛ inch thick) and, draw round the kaleidoscope with a pencil. Draw a smaller circle inside, about ⅛–³⁄₁₆ inch away from the outer line. Cut the ring shape out very carefully and accurately.

Smear adhesive round the ring and place it on a piece of Cellophane.

Cut up small pieces of coloured Cellophane and scraps of coloured foil from sweet wrappings. Drop them into the Cellophane backed ring. Cut a circle of greaseproof paper. Smear adhesive very carefully on the surface of the cardboard ring and smooth the greaseproof paper onto it, thus trapping the coloured scraps between the Cellophane and the greaseproof paper. None of the scraps should to able to escape.

Cut a piece of card 2½ inches deep by the circumference of the prepared ring and join the edges with Sellotape making a flush join.

Cover this section with a plain paper and slip it onto the tube. Twist the smaller tube as you look through the peephole and watch the patterns change.

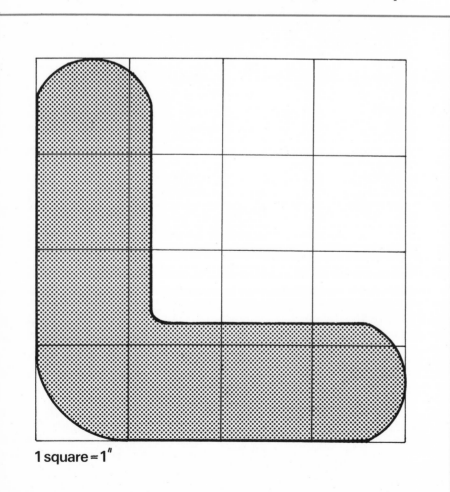

**1 square = 1"**

# 21

## Spinner hummer

Children can make spinners for themselves once they have been shown how, but it takes a little time for them to learn how to manipulate the tension of the strings and keep the spinner humming. For a really long lasting spinner, use hardboard but generally, stiff cardboard will do.

Cut a disc 3 inches in diameter. Drill or bore two holes 1 inch apart in the centre. Cut two 4 inch long handles from $\frac{3}{8}$ inch dowelling. Bore holes in the dowelling 1 inch from both ends. Thread twine through the disc and the handles. Knot the ends.

Paint an optic design on both sides of the spinner.

### To spin-hum

Hold the handles, one in each hand. Wind the string by spinning the disc on the twine with the right hand. Gently pull the hands apart and bring them together again while the twine twists and untwists. When the spinner is really going—it hums!

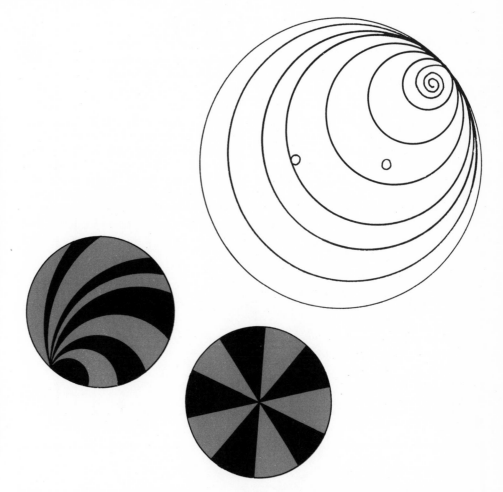

**21**. *Here is an optic design to trace off and paint on your spinner hummer and two more designs for you to try out. Paint them in bright colours* ▲

# 22

## Glider

A really efficient glider can be made from a sheet of writing paper and ordinary drinking straws.

The secret of the shape lies in clever folding, cutting and sticking.

Ideally, the sheet should be the International A4 size, that is, $11\frac{3}{8}$ inches deep by $8\frac{1}{4}$ inches wide. Use any fairly stiff paper if writing paper of these dimensions isn't available.

You will also need all-purpose adhesive, six straws and a paper clip.

Measure and mark the paper into thirds on one long side. Mark the points A and B. Measure one third and mark the measurement (approximately 4 inches) down from the top corners on both short sides. Mark these points a and b. Draw a line, joining A-a and B-b to form triangles on the corners. Cut both corners off and keep them for the nose section.

Draw a line dividing the paper in half

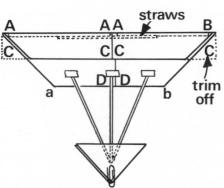

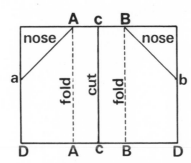

*Cutting and glueing construction for the notepaper glider* ▲

across the width. (C-c). Mark the two remaining bottom corners of the paper D and D.

Cut the paper in half along C-C.

Lay the two pieces of paper together as shown DC and DC and slightly overlapping. Glue and overlap.

When dry, fold the paper along the line A-A-B-B and trim off the corners that protrude. Glue three drinking straws along the fold. When the adhesive holding the straws has dried, fold the paper over them and glue round the edges.

Glue three drinking straws to the edge of the 'wing' as shown, with the other ends just meeting. Small pieces of Sellotape on the wing straws will hold them even more securely.

Glue the two nose sections together holding the three straw ends between them. Slip the paper grip into the point. Hold the glider on the central straw to launch it. The paper grip, is of course, on the nose end.

Decorate with camouflage designs or flight numbers if desired.

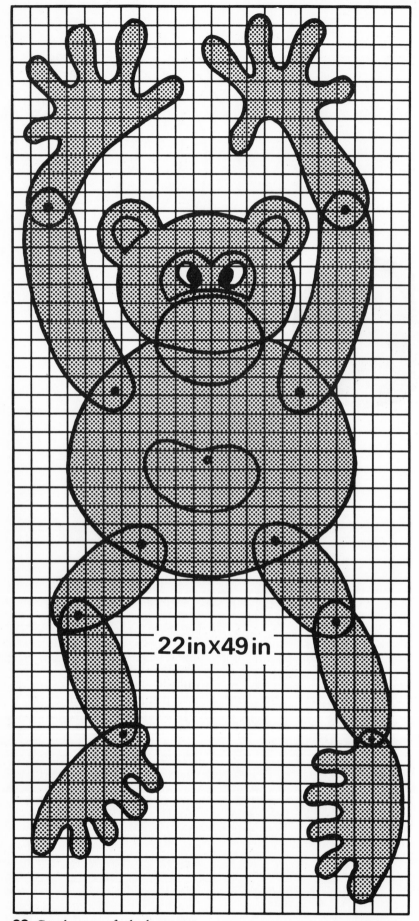

**23**. *Graph pattern for lanky puppet.*
*1 square = 1 inch*

22in × 49in

## Lanky puppet

A really delightful toy, jointed and lanky, to play with or hang from the nursery wall. Make the pieces in stiff cardboard by drawing up a pattern from the graph. Link the joints with brass paper clips—the kind that push through and open out on the wrong side.

For a long-lasting toy, cut the shapes out of hardboard and make the joints of small screws, washers and nuts.

## Character dolls

**Let children help you to make these delightful character dolls from the story of Red Riding Hood and then encourage them to try making dolls themselves, working freely and without following a pattern.**

Materials you will need:
Cardboard tubes
Coloured papers
Tissue paper
Gift wrap papers
Wallpaper
Scraps of felt, lace, ribbon, braid, bits of net, artificial flowers, short lengths of yarn, pipecleaners
Sellotape
Fabric adhesive
Paper adhesive

The character dolls illustrated were made on the cardboard tubes inside kitchen paper rolls, but if tubes aren't available, make your own by cutting lightweight cardboard (such as that used for cereal boxes), into 8 inch squares and rolling them into $2\frac{1}{4}$ inch diameter tubes. Join the tube with Sellotape.

Each of the dolls is made in the same way with paper cut to shape and built up over the tube in layers. Always work from the top of the head downwards. Cut paper longer and wider than you think you are going to need for a really good finish.

The arms of each doll are added when the rest of the doll is finished. Strips of card are cut to $3\frac{1}{2}$ inches long by $\frac{1}{2}$ inch wide, covered with paper and glued into position.

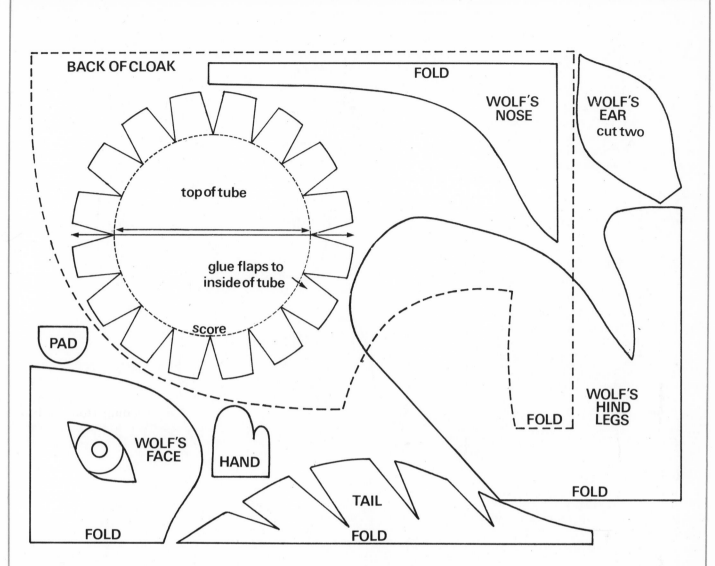

**24.** *Trace diagram for Red Riding Hood's cloak (shown as a broken line), and the wolf details. The circular shape is for the top of the tubes*

### Red Riding Hood and the Wolf
**The Wolf** Cover the tube with plain brown paper. Cut a strip 2¼ inches wide and long enough to go round the top of the tube from a different tone of brown paper. This is for the face. Allow sufficient when cutting for the overlap at the back.

Cut the features from the pattern, the face itself in white and the nose in black. Cut eyes and nose end as indicated. Add these to the head. Cut back legs and tail from black paper. Cover the arm strips with plain brown paper and add a black pad at the end of each. Fold the arms slightly before fixing them on to give the wolf a menacing look.

Cut two ears from felt, fold them into shape and glue to the head.

Make a wool fringe for the hair. Pierce three holes down each side of the nose and insert pipe cleaners. Glue them flat to the face.

**Red Riding Hood** Start at the head and cut a strip of pink paper 2½ inches deep for the face. Cut it long enough to go all round the tube with sufficient for overlap.

The dress is made from gift wrap paper cut long enough to cover the remainder of the tube and to slightly overlap the pink face. The hair is made from yellow wool, long enough at each side of the face to be tied into bunches. The hair is stapled to the top of the tube before the cloak is fixed on. Cut a pattern for the cloak and cut it out of red paper. Glue the cloak in position. Add a bow.

Cover arms with gift wrap paper, add felt hands and glue in position.

Add flowers or a basket for Grandma.

Make the eyes and mouth from scraps of felt. Eyebrows and cheeks are drawn in with a felt pen.

**Grandma** Make Grandma's face as for Red Riding Hood. Make her dress in the same way. The apron is made from a strip of net folded and glued to the dress. Cover the join with ribbon and tie in a bow at the back. Braid is glued to the sleeves and the bottom of the dress.

Glue felt decorations to the dress. The hair is made from double knitting wool and glued to the head. The top-knot is a plait of wool wound round and glued to the top of the head.

### Bride and Soldier
Use the same principle as for previous dolls and decorate as shown in the illustration.

# Wool scraps

Odds and ends of wool can be used in so many ways – for embroidering soft toys, for making decorative trims and for making all kinds of simple toys for young children. Try this simple technique for making a whole zoo of pompon animals.

## Pompon toys

Here's how to turn easy-to-make pompons into delightful little toys. By mixing two different coloured wools, the characteristics of birds, animals and insects can be achieved. A charming rabbit ball to hang over a cot for a new baby can also be made by the method described here.

Materials you will need:
Cardboard
Knitting wool
Scraps of felt
Fabric adhesive

Cut two cardboard rings to the diameter of the finished pompon. Cut a round hole in the centre of both rings, $\frac{1}{3}$ of the diameter. Both rings are worked together.
Thread a large needle with knitting wool. Double it but do not knot the ends. Wind the yarn over and through the hole until the rings are thickly covered with wool and the needle won't go through the hole easily. New lengths of yarn are joined in by holding the new length against the circle with a thumb and arranging the next two or three strands over the ends to hold them in place.
When the rings have as much wool on them as they will take, take a sharp pointed pair of scissors and holding the wool-covered rings with the thumb and first finger of the other hand, snip through the yarn strands on the edge of the circle.
The yarn will spring away from the card as you cut. Cut through all strands right down to the card. Cut off a length of matching yarn and slip it between the two cardboard rings. Tie a double knot tightly. Cut the rings away carefully. Roll the ball between the palms to make it round and trim all over with scissors to even up the pile.

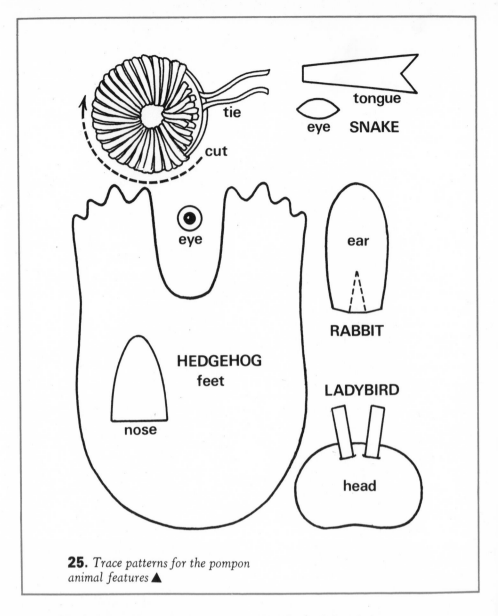

**25.** *Trace patterns for the pompon animal features* ▲

## To make pompon toys

Patches of second colour can be made in a pompon by winding one segment of the rings with the second colour. If this segment is worked first, directly onto the cardboard and until about eight layers of yarn have been worked up and the main colour is then worked round and over it, the second colour will come out as a round patch.
If some of the main colour is put down first, the segment worked on top, and then the main colour worked over that, the second colour will come out as two patches. Spots of colour can be worked onto a pompon in this way by arranging three or four segments.
Pompon toys have a base for the feet. Cut out the base from felt and glue the pompon down onto it. Cut out ears, eyes, noses, tails and glue them on. A rabbit will need a small white pompon for a tail. A pompon snake is made with six pompons in decreasing sizes threaded onto a length of matching yarn.

## Rabbit ball for a baby

Cut two circles of card 5 inches in diameter and cut the central holes $1\frac{1}{4}$ inches across. Wind white wool on one segment first and wind on about 8 layers. This is for the rabbit's nose. Wind pink or blue wool to cover the white segment and the remainder of the rings. Finish the ball off as before. Stitch a small white pompon ball on for a tail and two felt ears. Cut a length of narrow baby ribbon 30 inches long and stitch the two cut ends into the centre of the ball very securely from the middle of the rabbit's back. Loop the ribbon to make three or four loops each side of the central point. Stitch a small bell into the centre of the loops. The ball hangs from a pram canopy or just above the cot so that the baby can touch it with his hands and make it move but not pull it down into his mouth. The foot section is not needed for a hanging toy. If preferred, the tail and ears can be left off the ball – it looks just as pretty with just the ribbon.

# Cotton reels

In recent years, wooden reels have been gradually replaced with plastic ones. But you may find one or two of the wooden kind at the bottom of your workbasket and delightful toys can be made with them.

## Witch puppet

Marionnettes made from cotton reels can have heads made of stuffed socks but if you want to achieve a real character puppet, fashion the head from a modelling compound such as plastic wood or paper mâché. Whichever kind of head you decide upon, the main body string must go right through the head because the reels represent a considerable weight when the marionette is strung together and won't be supported sufficiently if the string is merely fastened to the top of the head.

Materials you will need:
Modelling compound for the head
Small beads for the eyes
Grey yarn for hair
Paints, green, red and black
Large black beads
Black and green felt
Black paper
Wooden stick 6 inches long
Few strands of straw
Black button thread
Black four-hole button
Thin black twine
13 reels, wooden or plastic
Strong adhesive
Fabric adhesive
Note: The twine must be of a thickness able to pass through the cotton reels and the beads twice.

Fashion the witch's head and give it a short neck. Just before the head is completely dry, push a matchstick or a cocktail stick right through.
Leave to dry thoroughly.
Paint the head green and the inside of the mouth red. Paint in eyebrows. Glue the small beads in position for eyes. Make the witch's hat from a three inch cone of black paper mounted on a circle of felt cut to fit the modelled head. Cut 2 inch lengths of yarn and glue them to the inside of the hat for hair.
Cut a 2 yard length of black twine and thread both ends first through the hat, then through the witch's head. Smear a little adhesive round the hair line of the head and push the hat on. Leave to dry. Paint the cotton reels black and dab a little colour inside the holes as well. Cut hands and feet from felt, green for the hands, black for the feet.

### Making the cloak
Cut the cloak from black felt. Cut the cape out and pink it all round the edges. Stitch the cloak under the back of the cape along A-A. Fasten the cape round the shoulders over the neck button and glue with fabric adhesive to close.

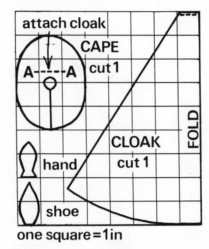

one square = 1 in

### Stringing the puppet
Leave a small loop of twine at the top of the witch's hat, held by a safety pin to stop it slipping through. One end of the twine needs to be very short, about six inches long. Pass the ends of the twine through diagonally opposite holes in the black button.
Tie the short end of twine to a safety pin. The long end of the twine is threaded through all the cotton reels and beads, following the diagram.
It goes first through the three body reels, then through a bead at the top of the right leg. Through the three leg reels through the foot bead and back up through the three leg reels. It then crosses over and goes through the bead at the top of the left leg, goes through three leg reels, through the left foot bead. Up through the left leg reels again and the top of leg bead again. Through the three body reels for the second time, through the bead at the top of the left arm and through two arm reels. The felt hand is stitched to the twine at this point. The twine then goes back through the arm reels, behind the shoulder bead and into the top right arm bead. Through the arm reels, sew the hand to the twine, back up through the reels, through the bead and knot the end to the end held by the safety pin.
Stitch the two foot shapes to the twine just above the foot beads.
Tie a length of button thread to the loop coming out of the top of the hat. Tie lengths of thread to each foot, between the hip beads and to each wrist. For simple control, tie the threads onto the edge of an old lampshade ring as shown in the diagram and control the strings with the fingers of the free hand. Make the witch's broom by tying straw round the stick and sewing one hand round the handle of the broom. A touch of adhesive will hold it fast.

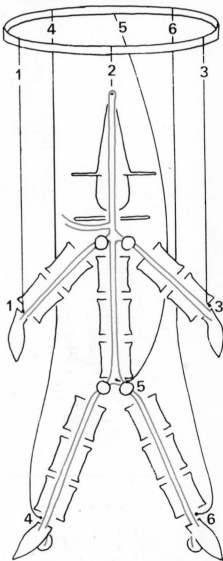

▲ *Stringing diagram: the lines show where the twine goes through the reels and beads*

All kinds of figures can be made by the method given here. The cotton reels can be painted or covered with patterned paper. If the figures are dressed in clothes, make the garments of very lightweight fabrics.

Cotton reels can also be used to make amusing models. Collect different shapes and sizes.

**Other things to make**

**To make a robot:** One large reel, two medium sized reels and two narrow thread spools. Glue together and paint.

**To make animals:** For most animals, one large reel and one medium sized reel. More of course for giraffes and crocodiles.

Thread pipe cleaners through the holes to join reels and bend the ends to stop them from slipping out. Glue bent pipe-cleaner legs to the underside of the body. Bend the ends again for feet.

**Horrible spider**. Paint a cotton reel black. Paint the pipe cleaners black.

Paint an evil face in white. Bend pipe-cleaners and push the ends into the hole at the bottom. Glue the legs to the edge of the reel.

**Soldier** Six medium sized reels. Glue one on top of another and paint. Cut a circle of felt and glue it to a circle of cardboard. Glue the felt side to the bottom reel.

# Cotton reel racer

A quick-to-make toy that a child will often find more fascinating than a model car. Try putting a small obstacle such as a pencil, in the racer's path – it climbs over it!

Materials you will need:
Wooden cotton reel
Two small panel pins
Elastic band
Short pencil or a 3 inch length of $\frac{1}{4}$ inch dowelling
Wooden or plastic bead
(Paint is optional)

Paint the cotton reel if desired.
Hammer in the two panel pins at one end, about $\frac{1}{8}$ inch from the edge of the hole and about $\frac{1}{2}$ inch apart.
Hook the elastic band round the pins and thread the remainder through the reel and then through a bead. Slip the pencil or dowelling through the elastic against the bead. Wind up the elastic by turning the pencil with a finger. Put the racer down on a smooth surface and watch it go!
A hint to help you thread the elastic. Pass a short length of thin twine through the loop of the elastic band. The twine goes through reel and bead easily and the elastic band follows after.

# Knitting Nancy

Knitting Nancys are one of the oldest of knitting toys and they are known all over Western and Eastern Europe, sometimes by different names. In Hungary, Nancys were sometimes carved into the shape of dolls and had faces painted on them.
A little girl will learn how to knit on a Nancy quite quickly and seeing the knitted tube emerge from the bottom of the cotton reel for the first time will be one of the most exciting things in her life.

Materials you will need:
1 large wooden cotton reel
4 panel pins approximately $\frac{5}{8}$ inch long
Knitting needle or cocktail stick
Ball of yarn

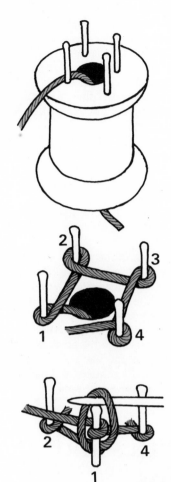

Clean the paper labels off both ends of the cotton reel. To make it pretty to use, paint the reel. Hammer in four nails about $\frac{3}{16}$ inch from the hole and in a square. About $\frac{3}{8}$ of the nail should be left showing.
Thread the end of the yarn through the hole in the reel so that a tail of about 6 inches hangs through.
Hold the Nancy in the left hand (if you

work righthanded).
With the right hand, wind the wool from the ball round each nail head in turn working clockwise.
When all the nails have one loop of yarn on them, wind the yarn round the next nail to the left once again. Hold the yarn with the left thumb and with the knitting needle, or whatever tool is being used, lift the lower loop of wool up and towards you over the upper loop and then off the nail, dropping the loop inside of the nail. Wind the wool round the next nail to the left and do the same again. Work round and round, winding the wool round the nail once and then lifting the loop underneath off. After about six rounds, pull the tail gently to start the tube through the hole but don't pull too tightly and get impatient to see the knitting appear or the tension will become too tight to lift the loops off easily. To finish off, break the yarn from the ball, thread the end onto a needle. With the needle, pick up each loop from the nails and tie them off together.

Although making a knitted tube is quite interesting to do and especially if random dyed yarn is used, some things can be made with lengths of knitted tube which will give a child an added incentive to keep knitting. For instance, make 12 six inch long tubes and stitch them together side by side. Mount them onto a square of felt for a pot-holder; a long length of tubing, about 24 inches, can be wound round and round and stitched into a mat for a teapot; three 24 inch lengths of tube sewn together will make an unusual belt – leave the last six inches on both ends of the tubes unstitched and hang a tiny bead or bell on each end. Lengths of tubes can be used as a kind of braid to decorate tote bags, boleros, hats, and the hems of jeans. Knit with raffia or Raffene for a different effect.

# Pop-gun

A simple toy to make which will shoot paper balls a remarkable distance.

Materials you will need:
Cork from a sherry bottle
An ordinary cork
Card, 6½ inches by 4 inches
Strong rubber band
Adhesive

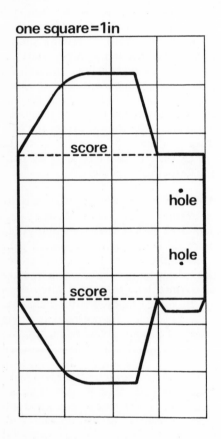

one square=1in

score

hole

hole

score

▼ *Cut this shape in paper*

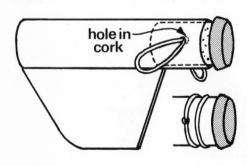

hole in cork

▲ *The cork and rubber bands fixed in position*

Cut the cap from the sherry bottle cork with a sharp knife. Glue it firmly onto the ordinary cork. Use a strong adhesive and allow to dry thoroughly.

Cut the shape given on the diagram from a stiff paper or lightweight card. Wrap the end of the cut-out shape that has the two holes round the cork and mark where the holes fall with a pencil. Make a hole right through the cork very carefully, taking care not to split it. A strong sharp needle will do the job. Push the rubber band through so that two loops of rubber band protrude each side of the cork.

Push the loops through the holes in the card. Note which way the cork faces in the diagram.

Loop the ends of the rubber band round the cap as illustrated.

Glue the small flap and the large flap together. The large flap makes a 'trigger' to hold the gun by.

To shoot the gun, drop a ball of paper into the barrel from the other end. Hold the trigger in one hand. Pull back the cork unit on the rubber band as far as it will go. Release – and pop!

# Fabrics and trims

Some of the fabric makes give 'scraps of fabric' or 'remnants of fabric' in the list of materials needed.

Fabric purchased from remnant counters is not always the most economical way of buying it. A piece labelled as 1¼ yard for the price of a yard isn't a good bargain if you only need ½ yard. You'd do better to buy exactly what you need from the roll.

If you enjoy sewing and making small fabric things, you'll find that one of the best sources of unusual and interesting fabrics is jumble sales. Buy up old clothes made of once-superb fabrics and unpick and rip out the best bits. Some really lovely printed fabrics can be obtained in this way for literally pennies. Bits of lace, beadwork and ribbon can also be acquired and are often of a far better quality than you can buy in shops, while the bead embroidery on old clothes can be a real source of decorative treasure. The colours of old beads are often far superior to the modern plastic variety.

# Baby balls

Balls made from fabric and felt are favourite gifts for babies and young children and with a bell inserted inside the stuffing, will give them hours of fascinating play.

If balls are to be washable, make them from cotton fabric scraps and seam the balls on the wrong side. Stuff them with small shreds of cut-up nylon stockings or tights (panty hose).

The balls illustrated are made on two basic shapes – the pentagon ball is ideal for felt patchwork. 26 pentagons make up a ball of the size shown and smaller balls will use fewer patches. Machine stitch the patches together or join with stab stitches.

The eight-section balls can be made up in cotton fabric, brushed nylon, nylon fur fabric or felt. Embroider small motifs on each section for a really pretty gift, or applique small felt motifs. For a different effect, cut each of the eight sections as two halves.

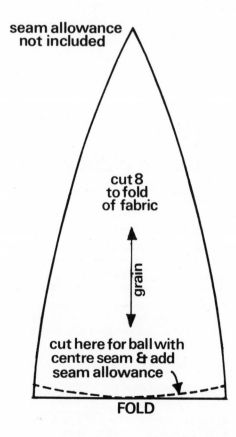

seam allowance not included

cut 8 to fold of fabric

grain

cut here for ball with centre seam & add seam allowance

FOLD

# 31

## Wigwam

As soon as the sun shines, you'll probably find your best sheet borrowed for a tent, draped over two garden chairs, a broom and a garden rake. A little hard on your good linen and not the best-made tent in the world! Make a wigwam from a worn-out single bed sheet and four garden canes – it will stay erect without collapsing and can be rolled up neatly and put away for another day.

Materials you will need:
An old sheet, single bed size
Four bamboo garden canes (at least 48 inches long)
6 yards white 1 inch tape
3 curtain rings
2 tins coldwater dye
Acrylic paints
(The dye and paints are optional)
The wigwam illustrated was made from a sheet which was dyed yellow and the Indian motifs were painted on after the wigwam was finished.

The wigwam is based on a half circle of fabric and the simplest way to cut this is to lay the sheet out on the floor, find the centre of the right hand long side and mark it with a pencil. Tie the pencil to a length of string and pin the end of the string to the point just marked. Put a kitchen weight on top of the pin to hold the sheet down while you draw out the half circle. Take the tied pencil in your hand and, starting at the top right corner of the sheet and holding the string taut, draw the arc until you reach the bottom right corner. On a single bed sheet this will give you a half circle with a radius of 50 inches.

The finished wigwam will stand approximately 4 feet high – big enough for children up to eight years old. To make a bigger wigwam, either use a double bed sheet and draw out the circle by the same method or cut a sheet up into four segments and join them, as shown in diagram B. This method of cutting a single sheet makes a wigwam approximately 70 inches tall.

Cut out the half circle of fabric. Using a plate as a template, cut out smaller a half circle in the middle of the long straight edge. On the wrong side of the fabric, draw a line from the centre point horizontally across to the edge of the half circle. Then bisect each of the quarter circles as shown in the diagram and draw in pencil lines. These lines are where casings are to be made for the canes.

The fourth cane goes onto a casing made on the straight edge above the centre point.

Make a hem on the bottom edge of the wigwam and along the upper edge.

The depth of these hems depends on the length of the canes. Bamboo canes vary in length and can sometimes be obtained as long as 5 feet. If only 4 feet long canes are available, adjust the hems so that 3 inches of the cane poke out at the top of the casing and 2 inches at the bottom. The overall depth of the wigwam after the top and bottom hems have been made would therefore be 43 inches.

### Making the casings
Pin and baste white tape along the pencilled lines. Turn the tape under at both end to neaten. Machine stitch on both edges of the tape. Leave the ends open.

### To make a closure
If the wigwam is to have a front which closes, sew three curtain rings to the right hand edge (this edge has the casing and care must be taken to see that the rings are not sewn through the casing itself or the canes will not go through). Sew six inch lengths of tape to the left-hand edge, to correspond with the rings. Slip the canes through the casings. Smear a little adhesive on the ends of the canes before inserting them. They will stick the fabric once they are in and will not slip out.

Tie the canes poking out of the top of the wigwam with twine and tie a bunch of feathers on. The wigwam will stand safely on its four legs but to make it more authentic and even safer, sew curtain rings at 12 inch intervals all round the hem. Use meat skewers for tent pegs. Push the skewers through the rings and into the ground.

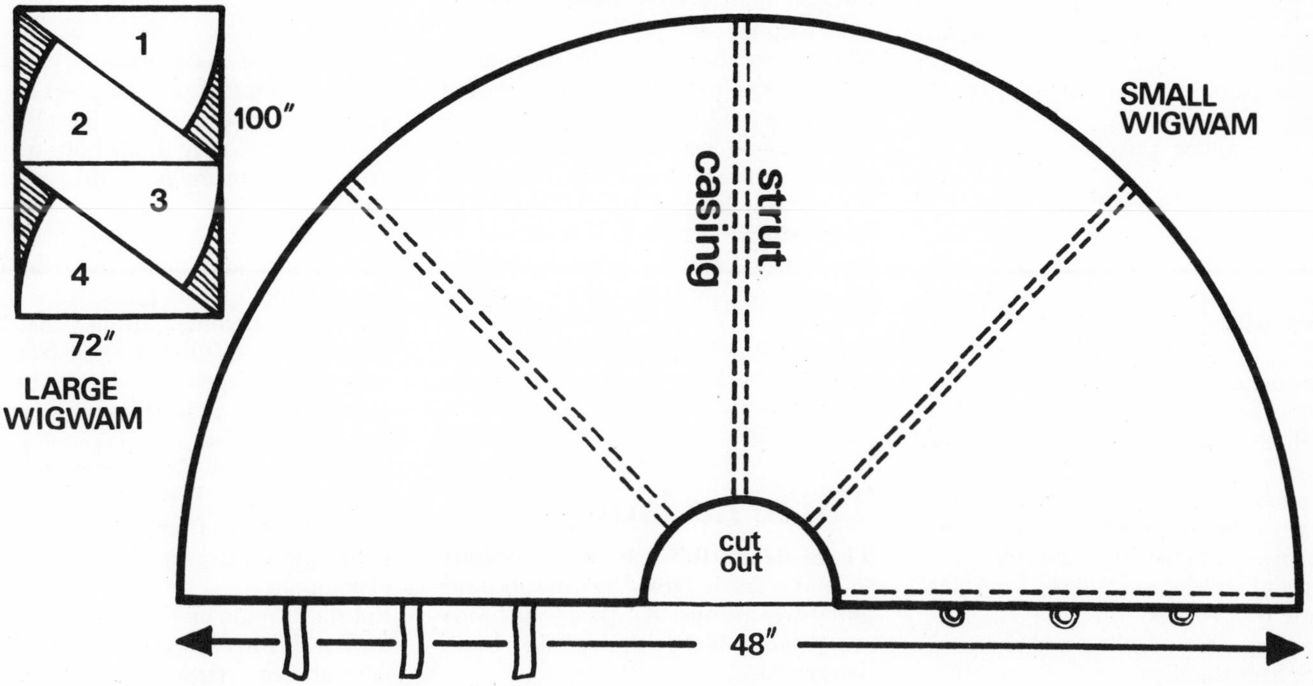

**LARGE WIGWAM** — 1 2 3 4 — 100" — 72"

**SMALL WIGWAM**

strut casing

cut out

48"

# 32

## Doll's sleeping tidy

**A child who worries about all the dolls and animals being warm and comfortable enough during the night will be re-assured by popping them into this practical yet pretty wall-hanging sleeping bag.**

Materials you will need:
1 yard sailcloth or cotton fabric
32 inches of gathered broderie Anglaise edging
60 inches broderie Anglaise edging
18 inch bamboo garden cane
Cotton remnants
Note: The broderie Anglaise edging is optional and if preferred, the sides can be finished off with self-fabric binding.

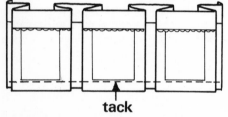

**tack**

▲ *Pleating the pocket section*

Cut a piece of sailcloth 28 inches deep and 24 inches wide. This is for the main part of the sleeping bag and makes the doll's bottom sheet. Turn a narrow hem to the right side on the top of this piece and then turn and machine stitch a 1¾ inch hem. This forms the casing for the cane rod.

For the pillows, cut out three pieces of patterned fabric with pinking shears. Cut each pillow 5 inches deep by 3¾ inches wide.

Pin, baste and then machine stitch the pillows to the main sleeping bag section, 10½ inches down from the hem, one centred and the other two 1½ inches away to left and to right.

### The pockets section

The pocket section of the sleeping bag has three little coverlets to match the pillows.

Cut a length of sailcloth 32 inches wide and 12 inches deep. On one long edge, turn a narrow hem to the right side.

Turn a 1½ inch hem and press. Insert the length of gathered broderie Anglaise under the edge of the hem and top stitch ⅛ inch from the edge.

Cut three coverlets from the patterned fabrics, one to match each pillow. Cut each one 6 inches deep and 4¾ inches wide. Pin, baste and then stitch the centre coverlet onto the pocket section first, placing it exactly in the centre, and 1 inch under the broderie Anglaise edging. Stitch the left and right coverlets in position, placing them 5½ inches away from the central coverlet.

To make the pockets, pin the central coverlet under its matching pillow, taking the pins through the pocket section to the main sleeping bag section. With the fingers, pleat the fabric each side of the central pocket, making pleats 1 inch deep. Pin the pleats. In the same way, adjust and make pleats at both sides of the right and left hand pockets. The coverlets should be positioned under their matching pillows. Adjust the pleats until they are. Unpin the pocket section from the main section but keeping the pleats pinned. Tack the pleats across the bottom edge of the pocket section and then machine stitch. Remove the pleat pins.

Join the pocket section to the main section across the bottom only, machine stitching, right sides facing.

Turn the sleeping bag to the right side and pin, baste and then machine stitch between each pocket from the bottom edge through the broderie Anglaise edging and to the pocket hem, stitching through both pocket section and the main bag section.

The sides of the sleeping bag are joined with rows of machine stitching on the right sides. The raw edges are afterwards bound with broderie Anglaise. Insert the bamboo cane into the casing. Cut two 8 inch long pieces of sailcloth to make loops for the two top corners.

Hang the sleeping bag from curtain hooks screwed into the wall.

# 33

## Three fat ladies

**Three delightful character cushions to make from fabric remnants and fancy trimmings. All three cushions are made from the same basic pattern.**

For each cushion you will need:
½ yard 36 inch wide fabric, needlecord, cotton, etc.
Small pieces of fabric for face, hands and general features
Bobble fringing for the hair or the wool to make pompons
½ yard of a firm, plain coloured fabric for the basic cushion shape inside
Foam chips or a similar filling

**KEY**
**a** neck line for A
**b** neck line for B
**c** neck line for C
**d** collar for A

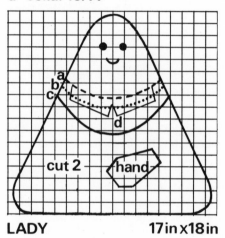

**LADY**      **17in×18in**

**To make the basic cushion**
Make a pattern from the diagram and cut out the inner cushion. Sew all round leaving a 5 inch gap in the bottom edge. Stuff and sew up the gap with oversewing stitches.

Cut out the outer cushion shapes. Cut out the face and hands from the pink fabric. Appliqué in place with zigzag machine stitching using matching thread. The features are cut from felt and glued in position. Place the two cushion pieces right sides together and sew all round leaving a six inch gap in the bottom seam. Clip corners and turn to the right side. The hair is made either from bobbles cut from a length of bobble fringe and sewn on individually or made of pompons.

Put the cushion on to the inner cushion form and either sew up the bottom seam or insert a zip fastener.

### Fat lady with flower (A)

Appliqué the collar just below the face before the two sides of the cushion are sewn together. The flower is cut out of felt and stitched in position.

A bigger smiling mouth and generous pompon hair completes the cushion.

### Fat lady with beads (B)

Two hands are overlapped and appliquéd in place.

A small length of strong thread is strung with beads and sewn in place when the cushion is completed. Make pompons for hair.

### Fat lady with cleavage (C)

A large pink face area is sewn on and a cleavage embroidered. Embroider very red lips and make small running stitches round the outline of the cheeks to give this fat lady a friendly look.

Cotton bobbles are sewn on for hair.

# Mermaid

**A glamorous sea-siren cushion to make for a day bed. Green satin from a discarded evening dress was used for the tail of the mermaid illustrated but any kind of fabric can be used, plain or patterned. If pink poplin isn't available for the body, dip-dye an old bed sheet.**

Materials you will need:
¾ yard pink cotton poplin
1 yard green satin or a similar fabric
3 yards looped fringe
1 cushion form
2 bags of kapok-type filling

Make a pattern from the diagram. Cut two tail pieces from the green satin, one front and one back up to the dotted line. Cut two body pieces from pink poplin and one arm.

Join the front body piece to the matching satin front and then join the tail piece on. Tack the arm in position and zigzag stitch round the outline.

Push some stuffing into the arm.

Make up the back by stitching the pink top to the centre back and adding the tail. Sew the two completed halves together leaving an opening at the centre bottom seam. Push stuffing in tail and head areas but do not stuff too tightly. Put the cushion form in the middle area of the body – this is where firmness is needed. Sew up the opening.

Embroider the eyes, or use a motif cut from a patterned fabric. Embroider the nose, using black embroidery thread and work the lips in pink. Sew on the fringing in three rows, to give the curled effect. Sew down loops round the face and leave two rows unsewn at the back of the head. Sew two flower motifs, stars or shells onto the bust.

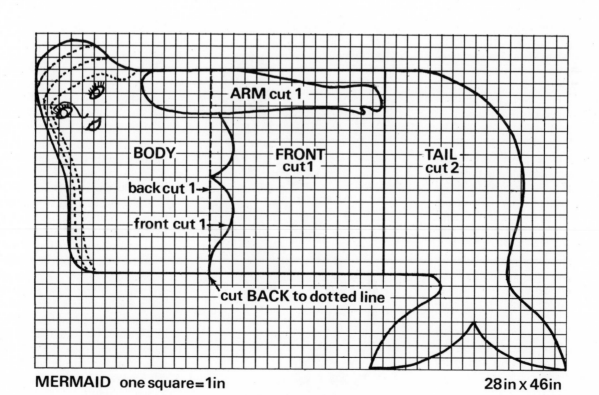

**MERMAID  one square=1in**                    **28in x 46in**

# 35

## Strong man

Cushions shaped like character people are top favourites with children and the strong man has a lot of appeal. Although satin is suggested for the body, any plain fabric can be used.

Materials you will need:
1¼ yards satin fabric 36 inches wide
½ yard 36 inch wide black fabric for the vest and boots
Striped ribbon for wrists and ankles
1 oz red wool for hair and moustache
Black embroidery thread
1 cushion form
1 bag kapok-type filling

Make a paper pattern from the diagram. Cut two body sections from the satin fabric, placing the pattern on the fold. Cut four legs from satin. Cut four boots and two vests from the black fabric.
Place the vest shapes onto the body sections and machine stitch or hand sew in place. Place the two body halves together right sides facing and stitch all round leaving the base open. Clip the curves and turn to the right side.
Stuff carefully, making the arms slightly bulgy. Pin the seam at the bottom temporarily.
Sew the boots together in pairs leaving the top edge open. Sew the legs together in pairs. Clip the curves and turn to the right side. Slip the boots onto the feet and catch stitch in place. Place the ribbon over the edge of the boot round the ankles and hand sew in position. Stuff the legs and pin into place in the bottom of the stuffed body. Sew across the base of the body taking stitches through the tops of the legs to hold them securely in place.
Embroider the features using black silk for the eyes and nose, red for lips and chest hair, using stem stitch. Cut eyeballs from a scrap of black felt and glue in place.
Make hair by cutting 30 strands of wool 14 inches long. Sew them down on the head with a centre parting and sideboards. The moustache is made from 12 strands 8 inches long and sewn into place under the nose.
The hands are stab stitched through with matching thread to indicate fingers. Sew wristbands round the wrists made from the remaining striped fabric.

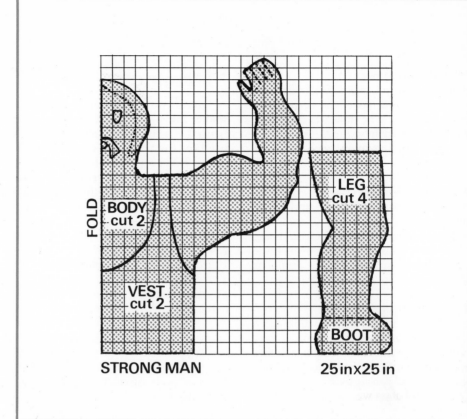

STRONG MAN — 25 in x 25 in

# 36

## Snake charmer

Charlie the snake charmer is a patchwork toy to make from scraps of fabric. He's the type of toy children hang around their necks or coil up and sit upon. The snake illustrated is approximately seven foot long.

### To make the snake
Cut pieces of fabric 11 inches wide and to any length over 8 inches. Seam the pieces together on the 11 inch sides. Cut the head piece to 11 inches square. Cut a forked tongue from red felt and pin it in position to the wrong side of the head section. Fold the snake along the length, baste and machine stitch, rounding off the head section and the tail. Leave gaps in the seam at about 15 inch intervals to make stuffing easier. Turn to the right side. Stuff very firmly with cut-up nylon stockings and tights – these make a good washable filling.
Stuff the head first and then work up the snake's body, closing the seams as you work.
Cut eyes from felt and glue onto the head.

# 37

# Bean bags

When you were a child, bean bags were soft toys to throw about and play catch with, rather like a kind of ball game. They were usually square shaped and one could manage some very tricky catches by grabbing a corner as the bean bag hurtled past.

Nowadays, bean bags are considered to be decorative toys and sometimes, a nice thing to cuddle for the very small. The baby seal bean bag for instance, made from soft jersey fabric, would make a delightful grab toy for a baby, if it were stuffed with foam chips instead of beans. Bean bags can be made to any shape at all – animals, birds, insects, fish, funny character people, flowers, vegetables – there is almost no limit. They can be made of felt, from fabric scraps or from leather and suede pieces.

It isn't necessary to use beans for filling – any of the pulses will do – lentils, split peas, dried peas and rice or pearl barley are good too. Remember that a bean bag filled with pulses or seeds cannot be washed. The filling must be emptied out first.

## Sitting hen

Cut the hen shape out of the fabric twice. Cut the comb from felt once and the beak once, cutting on the fold. Cut out two eye shapes.

Pin the comb in the position marked on the diagram on one hen piece, with the comb lying inwards towards the hen body. Fold the beak along the straight edge and glue the two surfaces together. Pin the beak in position, lying inwards to the hen body. Baste. Pin and baste the second piece of hen body fabric on top, right sides facing, with the comb and beak sandwiched. Machine stitch all round but leaving 2 inches unstitched on the underbody seam for inserting the filling. Turn to the right side and press lightly. Push some cotton wool filling into the hen's head and neck. Make a paper cone and pour in the split pea or beans filling. Don't fill the hen too tightly because she should bulge a little as she sits. Close the opening with over-sewing.

## Baby seal

Make the baby seal in the same way. Draw strands of black button thread through the head for whiskers. Run a knot up a pin so that it lies close to the fabric and cut the end off about ¾ inch long.

## Floozie doll

Fill the two legs with cotton wool first, packing the filling tightly near the toes and more loosely near the tops of the legs.

Fill the body with pea or bean filling from underneath. Insert the two legs into the underbody, pin and baste and close the seam with oversewing.

The graph patterns below can be scaled up to make large soft toys too. The baby seal, for instance, looks charming made to 20 inches long and in white nylon fur fabric.

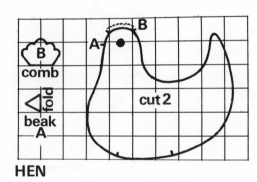

HEN

**37.** *Each of the three bean bags illustrated takes approximately 1lb of bean filling. Scale the patterns up for soft toys*

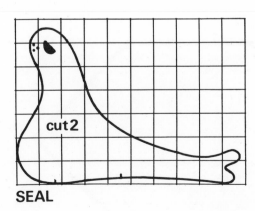

SEAL

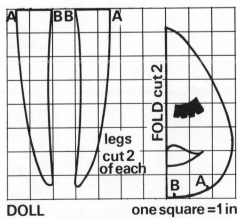

DOLL          one square =1 in

add ¼" seam allowance
on all main pieces

57

# Patch a quilt and cushion

Early American settler's wives hoarded every scrap of fabric and patched together beautiful quilts, some of which are collector's items today. Patchwork is enjoying a revival now – not only because it is a way of using fabric remnants, but because it is a satisfying form of creative sewing as well.

Children, with their love of colour and variety, appreciate patchwork. Quilts and coverlets with matching cushions are suitable for children's rooms and add a brilliant touch of colour to a simple decor. Large floor cushions, made to about a yard square, look particularly good, and 3 inch wide bands used to trim curtains give a co-ordinated look. Bathroom towels can be appliquéd with patchwork motifs and children's table mat and napkin sets look charming with a hexagon shape patched to one corner. Giant patchwork toys are great fun too. Make up large areas of patchwork and use the resulting fabric in the same way as one would use ordinary material, pinning the paper pattern in place and cutting the sections out.

Most needlework shops stock patchwork templates but the illustration shows how effective a simple square shape can look if strongly contrasting colours, fabrics and patterns are used.

### Making the patches

Using a template (you can make your own from the shapes given here), cut out the shapes in stiff paper. Strong brown paper or magazine covers are ideal. Using the template again, cut the shape out in fabric, leaving ⅜th inch turnings all round.

Pin the paper shape to the wrong side of the fabric (diagram A). Fold over the turnings and, starting with a knot, baste round the patch, using one stitch to hold down each corner. (Diagram B). Remove the pin (diagram C).

### Sewing the patches

Place two mounted patches together, right sides facing and oversew with tiny stitches along one edge. Start by laying the end of the thread along the top of the edge and sew from right to left over the thread.

Push the needle through the fabric at right angles so that the edges are neat and the patches do not stretch. To fasten

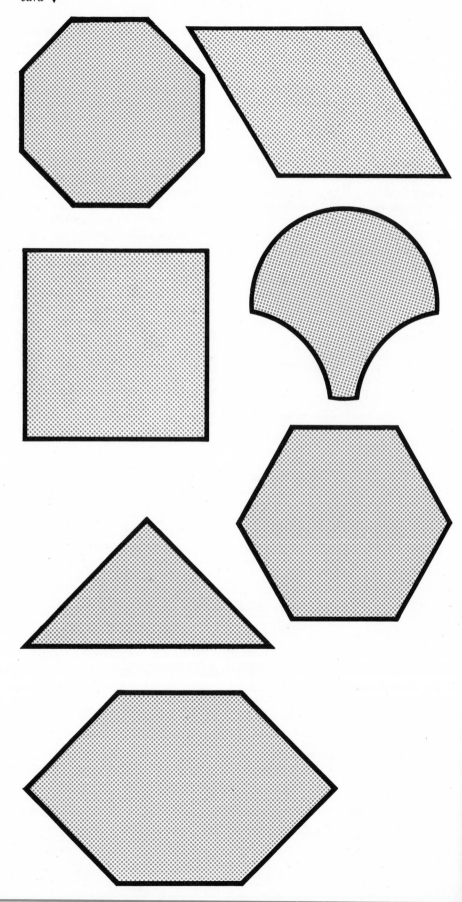

**38.** *Trace these basic patchwork shapes and make your own templates in wood or stiff card* ▼

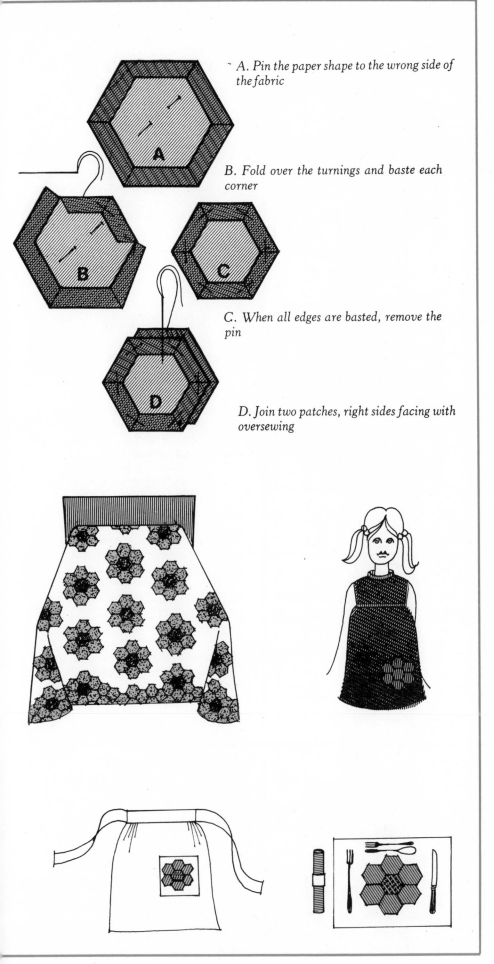

A. *Pin the paper shape to the wrong side of the fabric*

B. *Fold over the turnings and baste each corner*

C. *When all edges are basted, remove the pin*

D. *Join two patches, right sides facing with oversewing*

off, work back four stitches. Several patches can be joined continuously but make sure that the corners are firm by sewing one or two extra stitches over them.

**To finish off patchwork**
When all the patches are sewn together, press on the wrong side with a warm iron. Take out the paper shapes and tack round the outside edge of the piece of work to hold the turnings on the edge patches secure. The patchwork is now ready for mounting.

**Mounting**
Pin the patchwork in place and slip-stitch, using tiny stitches, all round the edge. Remove the edge tacking, press lightly just round the edge.
If the piece of patchwork is quite large, such as a quilt or coverlet, it will need to be caught through to the background fabric at various points – say every 9 inches or so across the area.

# Standing forest

One of the newest ideas for fun room decoration is cut-out standing trees, made of chipboard and painted with flowers and fruit motifs. Children will love having a miniature forest for themselves, made out of very stiff card or hardboard. Fix the base of the wide trunk to a 2 feet diameter base using a through housing joint.
Use the tree shape for a wall mural for a child's room too, painting the trees directly onto the wall behind the bed.

▼*Use this graph to make your tree any size you like*

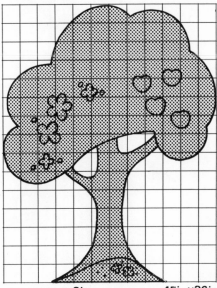

one square = 3in     45in×36in

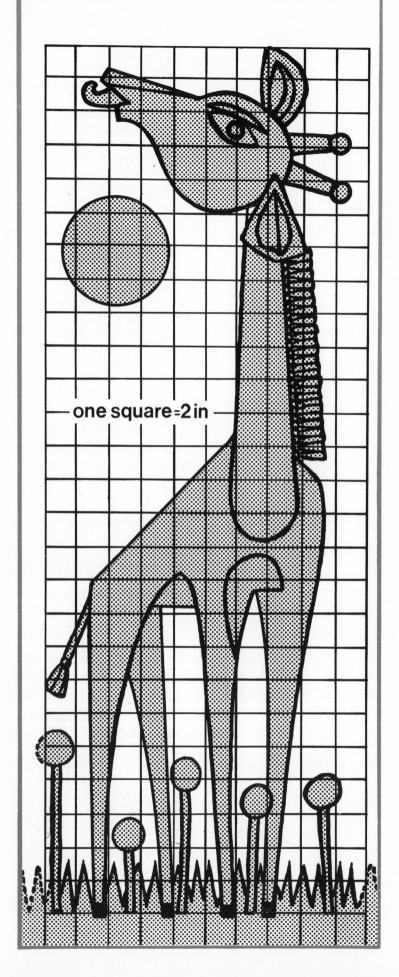

one square = 2 in

## Measuring hanging

Rather than mark the door jamb or the wall when measuring children's growth rate, make a colourful wall hanging from hessian, fabric and felt appliqué, and fasten a tape measure down one side. The giraffe hanging illustrated measures 58 by 22½ inches. Draw the giraffe outline from the graph and cut the animal's markings from fabric and felt scraps. Stick or stitch the shapes onto the background fabric.

How nice to be able to say, 'I'm almost as tall as a giraffe!'

## Doll's house

The doll's house illustrated was made from a cardboard box which had contained a knitting machine. The box was strongly made and measured 42½ inches high by 11¼ inches wide and 6¼ inches deep.
The floors of the house are made of strong cardboard and measure 11¼ inches by 6¼ inches.
A box of similar dimensions could be made from card or the house could be made of hardboard or plywood.

Materials you will need:
Box: 42½ inches by 11¼ inches by 6¼ inches
(or make a box to the dimensions given).
3 pieces of cardboard 11¼ inches by 6¼ inches for floors
**Exterior** Suitable fabric for covering the outer walls, a piece measuring 48 inches by 40 inches
Red felt for the roof; one piece measuring 20 inches by 8 inches; one piece cut in a triangular shape, 12 inches by 10 inches by 10 inches
**Interior** Fabric of suitable design for covering walls of the Kitchen, Living Room, Bedroom and Attic room. Each room will require a piece of fabric measuring 24 inches by 11 inches
Suitable fabric for floor coverings; 4 pieces measuring 11¼ inches by 6¼ inches
Lace or similar fabrics for curtains for each room
Fabric for rear wall 42½ inches by 11¼ inches
**Sundry materials** Odd pieces of black and white felt for exterior decoration.

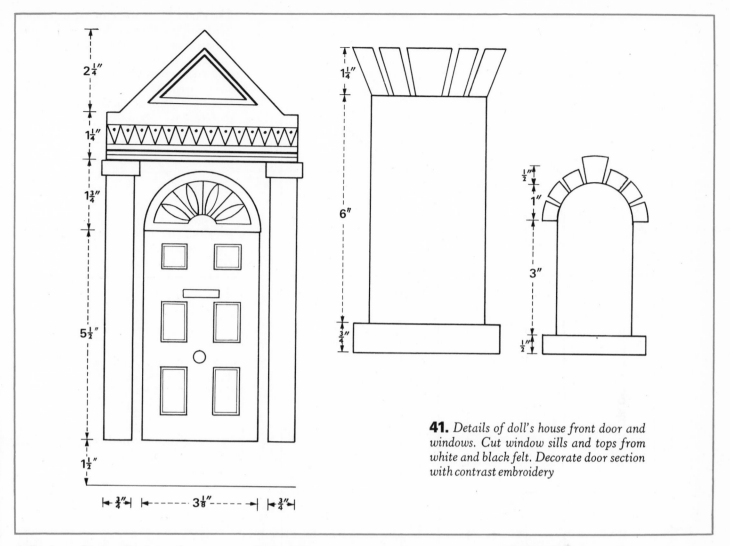

**41.** *Details of doll's house front door and windows. Cut window sills and tops from white and black felt. Decorate door section with contrast embroidery*

Adhesives: fabric adhesive, all-purpose adhesive
⅛ inch wood dowelling
Beads
Wire
Cellophane or acetate film

## Construction

Check with diagram for measurements if the outer is to be constructed from card, hardboard or wood.

1. Draw out the Back, Side, Front, Side. Cut out windows and the shaping of the front and rear walls with a sharp knife. Three sides of the door are cut, the remaining side being scored so that the scoring acts as a hinge and the door opens inwards.

Score all folds in the cardboard and strengthen all folds with sticky backed fabric tape or strips of thin cotton glued to the inside of the fold.

2. Cut three pieces of card for the floors, 1 inch wider and 2 inches longer than the actual size. Fold the extra on each piece of card, snip into the corners and glue the floors to the walls to secure. The side of the floor at the back of the house does not need the extra inch as the back of the

house opens.

Strengthen the join of floors to walls with sticky backed tape or glue strips of thin cotton fabric to make them secure.

3. The roof sections are folded inwards. Glue the sections at the ridge and to the front wall using sticky backed fabric tape or glue strips of fabric (As the exterior walls and interior walls will be covered with fabrics, the strips of fabric used for strengthening joins will not show when the house is finished.)

Cover ceilings with suitable fabrics and make light fittings by threading beads onto wire and inserting the wire through the ceilings.

Glue down the floor coverings.

## Exterior

The exterior fabric on the doll's house illustrated was cut in one piece and cut about 3 inches larger all round to allow for turnings to the inside. If this seems to you a difficult way to handle the outside covering, cut the fabric for each section separately, but make sure that sufficient fabric is allowed for covering corners and for turning to the inside. Cut into the fabric for the roof section

to be fitted later.

Cut away the fabric from the doors and windows. Turn the edges to the inside and glue them to the inside walls neatly. Glue Cellophane to the inside of each window. Make sure that sufficient margin is cut all round.

Cover the roof sections and the triangular shape of the rear wall with red felt cut exactly to size.

The window sills are made from white felt. The top of each window is a piece of black felt with white felt shapes glued on. The door fanlight is made from white and black felt decorated with stitching.

## Interior

Cut the fabrics for the walls of the rooms. Cut the pieces very accurately and with clean edges to window and door openings. Glue them in position. A length of dowel rod is fixed across the windows from side to side of the living room and bedroom. A small pin inserted from the outside at each end will hold it in place. Make full curtains and hang them from rings. Make a pelmet from card and fabric.

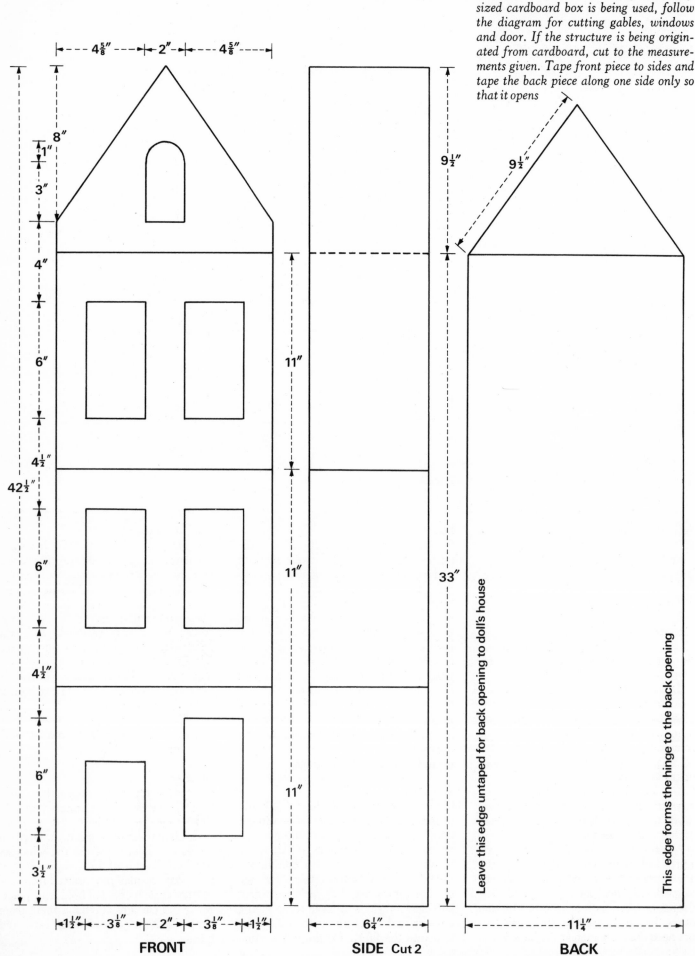

**41.** *Doll's house structure. If a suitably sized cardboard box is being used, follow the diagram for cutting gables, windows and door. If the structure is being originated from cardboard, cut to the measurements given. Tape front piece to sides and tape the back piece along one side only so that it opens*

4⅝"  2"  4⅝"

8"
1"
3"
4"
6"
4½"
42½"
6"
4½"
6"
3½"

9½"
9½"

11"
11"
33"
11"

6¼"

11¼"

1½"  3⅛"  2"  3⅛"  1½"

**FRONT**

**SIDE** Cut 2

**BACK**

Leave this edge untaped for back opening to doll's house

This edge forms the hinge to the back opening

# Christmas tree decorations

Christmas tree decorations are more fun if they're home-made and children can join in the making. Cut shapes out of cardboard – some are illustrated but trace some more from book and magazine illustrations. Cover the shapes with felt, inserting a small loop of thread before glueing.

Decorate the shapes lavishly with beads, buttons, sequins, scraps of lace and braid. Dab adhesive on some areas and sprinkle glitter dust onto them.

Decorations can also be made with the cornflour and salt modelling mixture described on page 113. Roll the paste flat with a rolling pin – about $\frac{1}{4}$ inch thick – and cut out shapes with Christmas cookie cutters.

Insert a thread loop in one end and leave to dry overnight. Paint with poster paints.

Another easy-make for children to try. Collect fir cones, twigs, dried leaves, wishbones, nutshells and egg-shells. Paint with gold water paint and sprinkle with glitter dust before the paint dries.

# Giant doll

Children adore big, friendly toys and this doll is likely to become someone's best friend. Working to the scale given the doll will stand 4 feet tall and could be dressed up in a child's discarded clothes.

The pattern can be scaled up or down to make dolls big and little.

Cut the pattern shape out twice in a firm cotton fabric. Baste and stitch, wrong sides facing, leaving an opening under one arm for inserting the filling. Almost any kind of stuffing material will do – old stockings, tights or synthetics cut into strips or pieces make a good, soft and washable filling.

Insert a short length of dowelling into the head and neck as you stuff so that the head doesn't flop too much.

Embroider the features with wool and make the hair from short lengths of wool. Dress the doll in clothes made from fabric scraps or in discarded children's clothes.

To make smaller dolls, draw the pattern to a different scale. For instance, for a 12 inch doll work to a scale of 1 square equalling 1 inch. To make a tiny clutch toy for a baby, use a scale of 1 square equalling $\frac{1}{2}$ inch.

# Wall tidy

An easy-to-make wall tidy to encourage a child to put things away. Use fabric remnants for the pockets and if large enough rings are difficult to find, cut cardboard rings and wind white twine, raffia or knitting wool to cover the ring.

Cut eight pieces of contrasting cotton fabric for each wall tidy, 10 inches deep by 7 inches wide. Seam them together on the long side to make first a strip and then a ring. Make a single narrow hem on one long edge and machine stitch. Turn a 1 inch hem and catchstitch down. Turn the circle inside out and fold it flat so that there are four squares of fabric on the under section exactly matching four squares on the top section. Baste and then stitch the raw edge at the bottom of the folded strip together. Still working on the wrong side, machine stitch the two thicknesses together to make four pockets, stitching exactly on the seam lines between the four squares.

Stitch rings to the middle of each pocket on the back piece and hang the wall tidy from hooks.

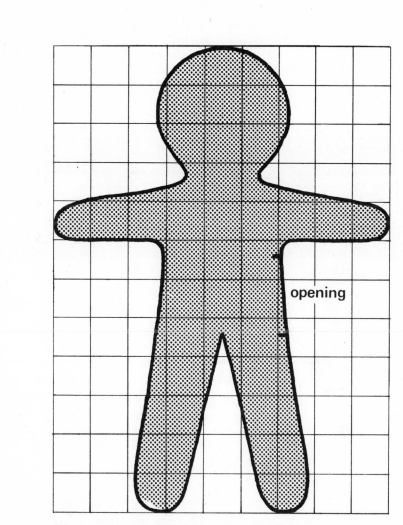

**43.** *Graph pattern for the giant doll. For a 4 ft doll, 1 square = 4 inches*

# Fairy cottage lamp

A charming bed-side lamp for a child's room, made to look like a little cottage. The light glows through the windows showing that Mrs Twitchet is at home and when the lamp is switched off she has gone to bed – and it's time the young owner did too!

For absolute safety, the lampshade should be made of a fireproofed material such as plasticised roller blind fabric. A low wattage bulb should be used in the lamp and the hole at the top of the shade should be at least 4½ inches in diameter.

Materials you will need:
Drum shaped lampshade frame
Plasticised roller blind fabric
Black enamel
Acrylic paints
Plastic straws
Adhesive
12 inch square of 1 inch wood for the base
Flanged wall-mounted bayonet fitting
½ inch wide white tape

Cut a strip of the fabric to fit the circumference of the frame plus one inch for overlap.
Bind the entire frame with cotton tape.
Plan and draw out the exterior details of the cottage on the right side of the fabric – windows, doors, beams etc. Hold the fabric against a window and draw the window areas on the wrong side.
Paint the wrong side of the fabric black but leaving the window areas unpainted.
Paint the exterior cottage details with acrylic paints.
Cut a circle of fabric to the diameter of the lampshade plus 1 inch all round. Cut a hole in the centre 4½ inches in diameter. Cut a segment from the ring, approximately 2 inches wide at its widest point, so that when the edges are re-joined and glued, the roof slopes slightly and the circle fits the top of the lampshade frame.
Glue the walls to the frame, joining the overlap. Glue the roof to the frame. Paint the roof brown. Glue lengths of straws to the roof for thatch and paint brown too.

**To make the lamp base**

Paint the wood base. Drill a hole in the centre for the lamp flex to go through. Cut a channel from the hole to the edge of the wood for the flex so that the wood base stands level. Screw the lamp fitting to the wood.

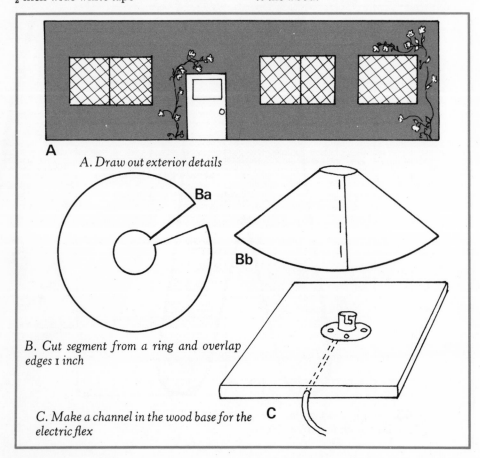

A. Draw out exterior details

B. Cut segment from a ring and overlap edges 1 inch

C. Make a channel in the wood base for the electric flex

Make a child a world of his own with a
play plan rug

## 47

(Left) A doll to teach tinies to button, zip and tie knots

## 48

These felt boots are made for giving

## 49

(Above) '. . . and they lived happily ever after.' Finger puppets to tell the story of Cinderella

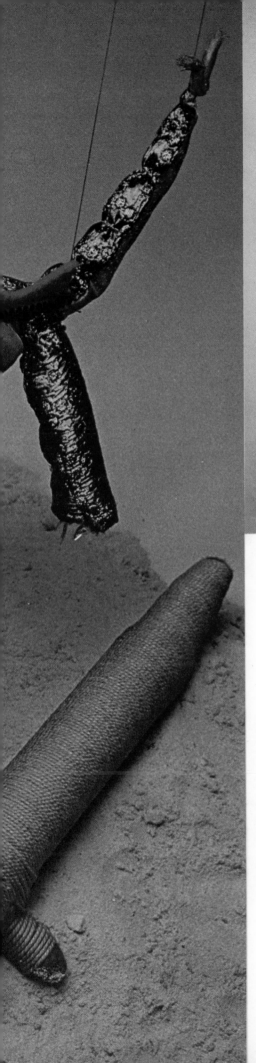

# 50

(Left) String and paper animals with a prehistoric look

# 51

Slinky cork snake slithering through the sand

# 52

A fabulous, glittering dragon marionette flies in on the scene

# 53

(Above) Some paper plates and a bit of paint – have a lot of fun !

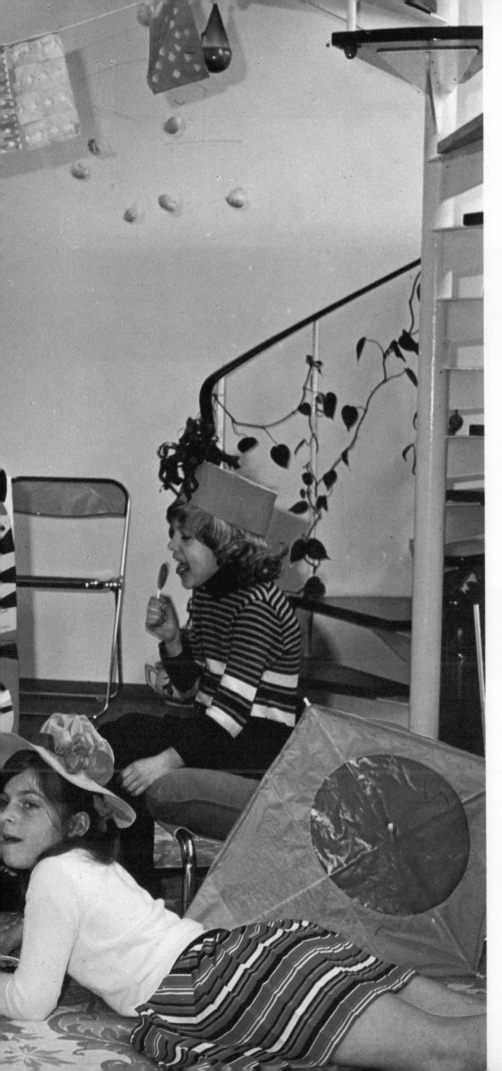

71

**59**

*(Left) A new way to tell the Christmas Story*

**60**

*(Above) Smartie-party centrepiece*

74

65

*(Left) A sunlit farmyard in papier mâché scaled to fit toy animals and figures*

66

*(Above) The enemy lands in a small fishing village. Battlefield to make in papier mâché*

67

*(Left)* Peek-a-boo pop-up toys to amuse a baby

68

*(Below)* Painted cans to keep a nursery desk tidy

**69**

(Left) Tin-can tanker truck to push along the floor

**70**

Anyone for golf? Play it indoors or out

**71**

Take a tin can, a rub of resin and listen to the hen cluck

**72**

Can you walk on stilts? On these cans you can

**73**

(Above) A Hottentot from an old sock

**74**

Up to the elbow in stocking snake

**75**

Savings sock to make for small change

**78**

*Win or lose, bagatelle is fun to play*

**79**

*A sweet doll's carrycot made from a
shoebox*

**76**

*(Below) Newsprint draughts (checkers)
board and bottletop counters*

**80**

*Simple box loom on which to weave a host
of things*

**77**

*(Right) Count the days to Christmas
with this bottletop advent card*

**81**

*Put your eye to the peephole and enter the
magic world of cinema*

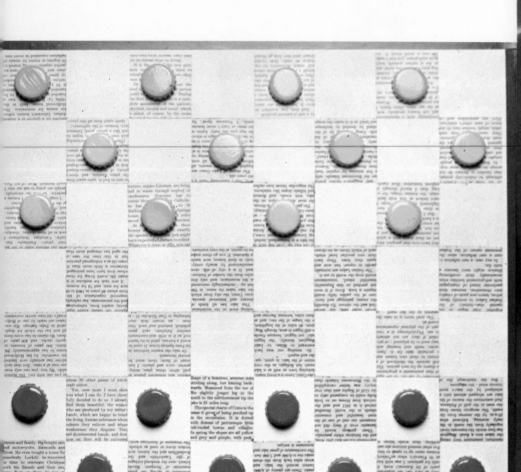

**82**

*(Below) Everything's coming up lovely in this window-sill garden*

**83**

(Right) Nutshell ladybirds to play games with

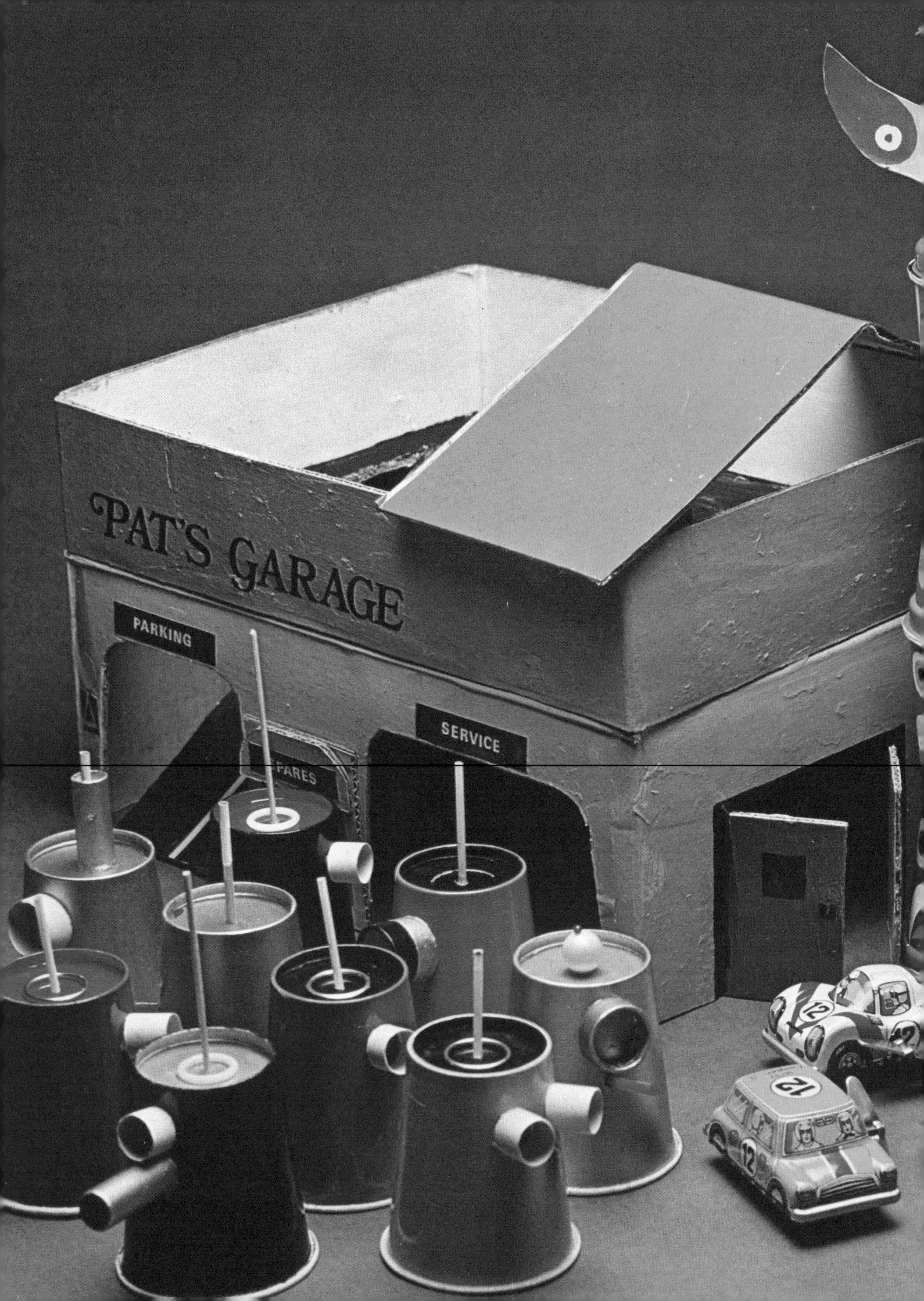
PAT'S GARAGE
PARKING
SERVICE
SPARES
12

# 84

(Left) Make this two-storey garage from a cardboard carton

# 85

The Martians have landed. Exterminate the Earth men!

# 86

A lot of hocus pocus with a brightly painted totem pole

# 87

Quoits or hoop-la? Take your pick

# 88

(Above) A spare fruit punnet? Turn it into this pretty workbasket

(Below) Roll a ball and with a bit of
luck, strike first time!

(Right) Mrs Murphy, dressed and ready
for market

**97**

*(Left) Everything but the kitchen sink makes this amusing collage*

**98**

*Wooden-top dolls to make from clothes-pins*

**99**

*(Below) Miniature furniture from matchboxes*

**100**

*Ta-ra, Ta-ra, Ta-ra, here comes the toytown band!*

# Instructions for designs 46-101

## Play Plan

The play rug illustrated is made of hessian, fabric and felt appliqué and embroidery and, although it is a major sewing project, would make a superb and long-appreciated gift for a child. Follow the key for the major areas on the plan. The finished rug measures 36 inches by 54 inches. The rug can be made up as a wall hanging by sewing 1 inch brass rings along one edge on the wrong side.

For table-top play, draw out the play plan to half scale on cardboard or stiff white paper – cartridge paper is ideal. Indicate the different shapes in pencil and let a child cut up sticky-backed coloured paper or paint the areas with his own paints. You might supply him with odds and ends of felt and fabric, small buttons, beads and ends of yarn and string and suggest that he glues them down for flowers, trees, ponds and fences.

Materials you will need:
1½ yards 72 inch wide hessian, in deep sea green
6 yards 1 inch wide wool braid, in navy
Ricrac braid: 2 yards white, 3 yards emerald, 1½ yards yellow, ½ yard red
4 yards ¼ inch wide white tape
8 yards 1½ inch wide beige webbing

Guipure lace daisy edging; 2 yards white, ½ yard pink
½ yard 36 inch wide turquoise fabric, for sea
½ yard 36 inch wide felt, orange
12 inch squares felt in dark brown, mid brown, maroon, lime green, leaf green, apricot, flesh pink, pale yellow, cerise pink and sand brown
Scraps of felt in red, grey, olive green and white
Scraps of four flowered fabrics
Thin foam, 36 inches by 54 inches
Soft embroidery thread in white, beige, pink
Fabric adhesive

### To make the rug

Cut the hessian into two pieces, each 36 inches by 54 inches. Bind the raw edges of one piece with narrow adhesive tape to prevent fraying. Keep the remaining piece for backing the completed rug.
Major pieces are pinned, tacked and stitched in place one at a time. Cut out the sea from turquoise fabric, allowing plenty of underlap to go beneath bridges and beaches. Machine stitch in place, using zigzag stitch if possible, or a straight machine stitch ⅛ inch from the edge.

### To complete the rug

Remove the adhesive tape binding. Press the rug lightly. Dab adhesive over one side of the backing hessian. Smooth the foam padding over the glued side of the hessian, working from the centre towards the edges. Dab adhesive over the foam. Place the rug over the foam, right side up, and tack round the edges through all three thicknesses. Press the wool braid in half lengthways, tack one edge over the right side of the rug, mitring corners. Stitch. Turn the other edge of the braid over to the wrong side of the rug, slip stitch. Cut the remaining braid into four equal lengths. Make loops and stitch them to the wrong side of one long edge. Use the loops to hang the rug on the wall when not in use, or stitch on brass rings.

### Key to appliqué areas

Sea – Turquoise coloured fabric
Roads – Beige webbing
Airport runway – Orange felt
Grass – Green felt
Hangar – Maroon and pink felt
Fields – Dark brown, mid brown and green felt
Gardens – Flowered fabric scraps
Houses – Different coloured felts
Trees – Brown felt for trunks, green felt for foliage, fruit from various coloured felts
Treasure island – Sand brown, green and orange felt

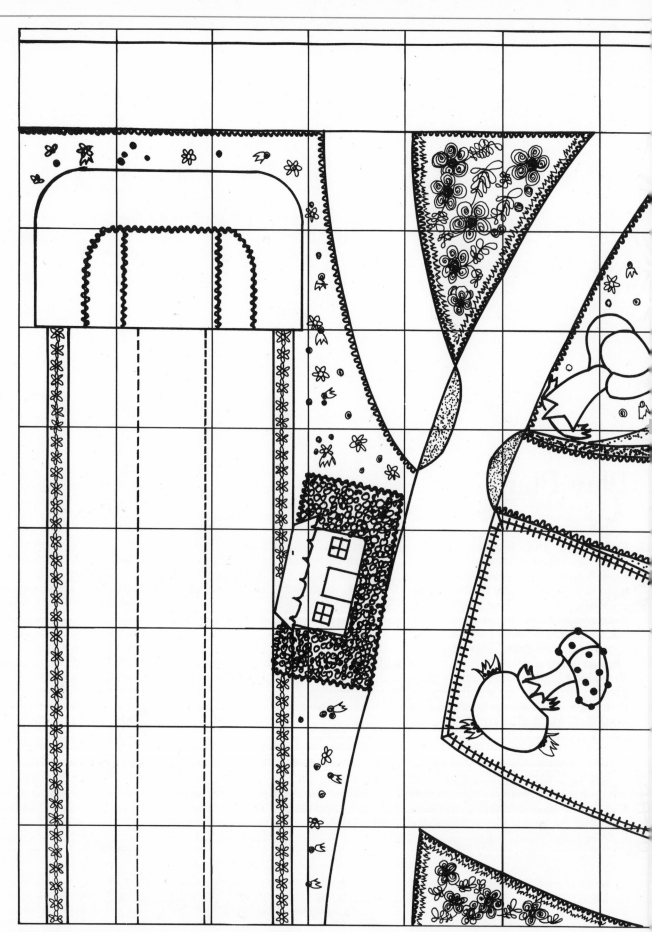

**46.** *Graph pattern for the floor play plan. Draw each square up to 2 inches to make a full sized floor rug or wall hanging. Work to a smaller scale for a table top game for a child to colour*

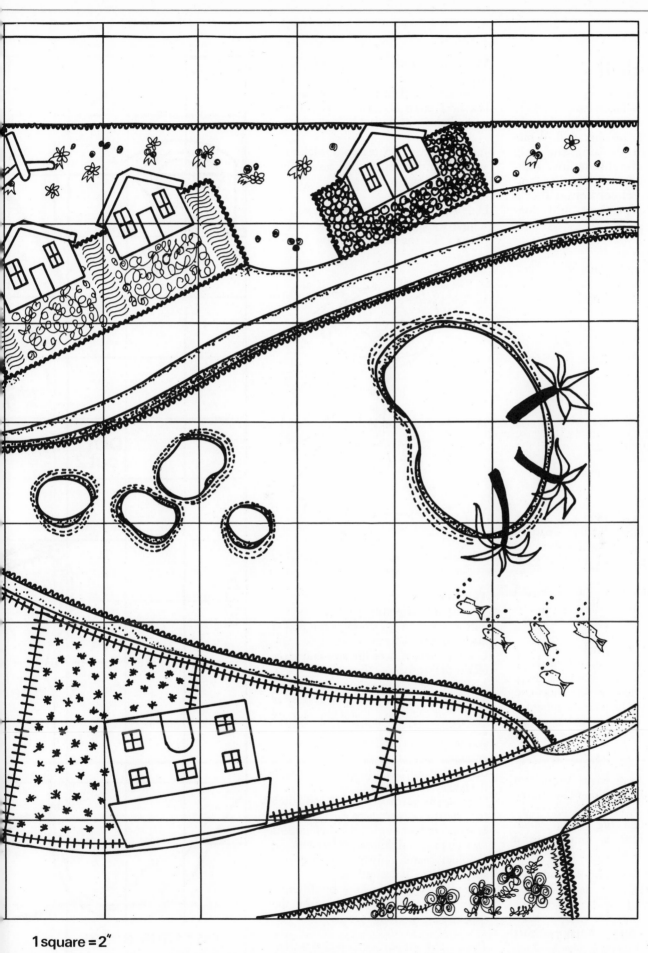

1 square = 2″

# Teacher doll

Learning how to do up his buttons and tie his shoe laces can be made much more fun for a small child with the help of a teacher-doll. While undressing and dressing the doll, children learn about fastenings without being aware of learning and when nursery school comes they'll feel more independent and confident.

Materials you will need:
Pink fabric, soft and washable
Nylon rugwool for hair
Stranded embroidery threads
Foam chips
Fabric for dress
Fabric for half petticoat
Fabric for waistcoat
Felt for jacket
Bias binding
Press studs
2 1 inch buttons
Hooks and eyes
12 inch cord or twine
4 inch zip fastener
12 inches 1 inch wide ribbon

## Making the doll
Cut the doll shape from a pink, soft and washable fabric using a pattern made from the graph. Stitch all round on the wrong side and fill with foam chips.
Make hair from nylon rug wool and stitch to the head. Embroider the features.

## Fastenings on the clothes
**Button-up dress** Cut a strip of fabric 30 inches wide and 10 inches deep. Make a narrow hem on one short end and turn a 1½ inch hem on the other for a front facing. Gather one long edge on a 12 inch strip of bias binding to fit the doll's neck. Neaten the ends, sew on a small press stud. Make a hem on the remaining long edge. Work two vertical buttonholes either by zigzag machine stitch or hand sewing, working right through the facing. Stitch on two large buttons to correspond with the button holes.

## Half petticoat with hook and eye
Cut a strip of fabric 18 inches wide by 5 inches deep. Join the short ends for 4 inches. Make a narrow hem. Gather the top edge of the petticoat onto a waistband made of bias binding. Stitch on a hook and eye.

**Waistcoat with lace-up fastening** Make the waistcoat from felt. Pierce eyelet holes and thread through a shoe lace or a piece of cord. Finish off the eyelet holes with buttonhole stitches.

**Jacket with a zip fastener** Make the jacket from felt. Stitch in a heavy duty zip fastener by hand.

**Hair bow to tie** Fold a 12 inch strip of 1 inch wide ribbon. Stitch the fold to the hair. Tie the ends into a bow.

## Teacher book
The same principle of teaching to button and lace up works if the doll is made up in book form.
Use the pattern here life size and trace off the doll and the clothes.
Make the pages of the book first from a firm fabric – closely woven cotton is ideal. Cut each page 10 inches deep by 8½ inches wide. Trace the doll's outline and features on each page and embroider them. Use stem stitch for working the outline. Stitch knitting wool through the fabric for hair.
Cut out the garments in felt and stitch the relative fastenings to each garment. Sew one garment only onto each outline on each page, stitching on side seams and shoulder seams only. Trim away any surplus felt to fit the outline.
Make the pages into a book by stitching down the left side, ½ inch away from the edge and using strong thread.

*Trace and graph pattern for teacher doll* ▶

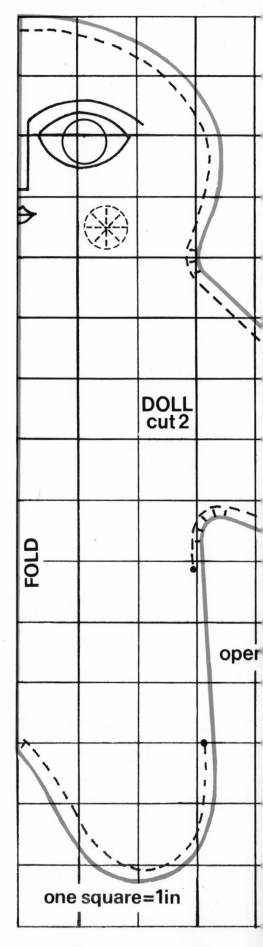

DOLL cut 2

FOLD

open

one square=1in

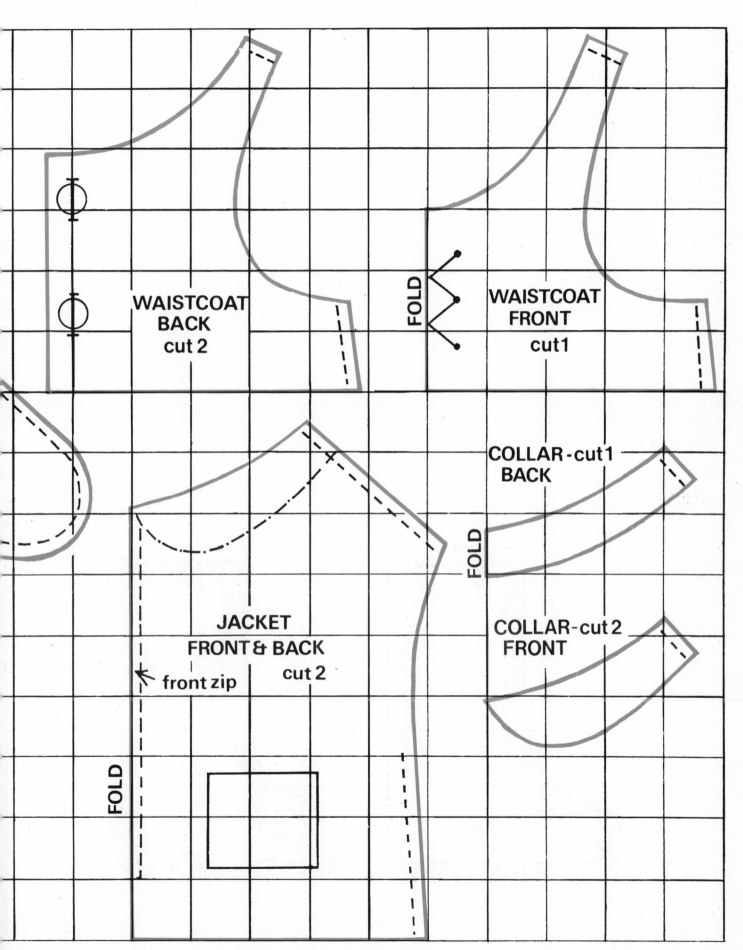

WAISTCOAT
BACK
cut 2

FOLD

WAISTCOAT
FRONT
cut1

COLLAR-cut1
BACK

FOLD

COLLAR-cut 2
FRONT

JACKET
FRONT & BACK
cut 2

front zip

FOLD

# Christmas stockings

Decorative Christmas boots or stockings made of felt make even the simplest gift look more exciting. The two stocking patterns here are styled so that they can be used after Christmas as hanging 'tidies'. A brush and comb or six pairs of rolled up socks would fit neatly inside.

Materials you will need for each boot:
Felt, 14 inches by 20 inches
Mercerised sewing thread
Embroidery threads
Curtain ring
Beads, braids, ribbon scraps
Fabric adhesive

### Making the basic stocking

Draw a paper pattern from the graph, working to a scale of 1 square to one inch. This will produce a stocking 14 inches deep with a mouth of 6 inches across. To make a larger stocking, adjust the scale. For instance, if you work so that 1 square equals $1\frac{1}{2}$ inches, the finished stocking will measure 21 inches deep with a mouth 9 inches wide.

Make two tracings from your pattern; one is used for transferring the design to the stocking. The second is cut up into the various components of the design and is used for cutting out the felt shapes.

Cut out the basic stocking shape twice in felt. The stocking is made up after the decoration has been completed.

### Decorating the stocking

Transfer the design onto the cut out stocking shape. Dressmaker's carbon paper is used but if this is not available, rub chalk onto the back of the tracing. Draw over all the lines of the design with a sharp pencil, making sure that all the guide lines you need for placing the felt pieces are clearly marked. Decide on the colour scheme for the design. Write the name of the colour on each section of the design on the tracing. Cut up the tracing, separating each section which is to be in a different colour.

Pin the paper shapes onto felt and cut each piece out very carefully. As each felt shape is cut out, place it in position so that you can see instantly if a colour needs to be changed for another.

When all the pieces of the design have been cut out and arranged, glue each piece down with fabric adhesive. This will hold the felt securely but for an even better finish, stitch the shapes too with small stab stitches all round the edges or work machine zigzag stitch. Wait until the adhesive is quite dry before sewing. Add the decorative touches, braid, lace, beads, ribbons etc., last of all.

### Making up the stocking

Place the two stocking sections together wrong sides facing and pin and tack. Seam with small stab stitches, working very close to the raw edge or machine stitch. Matching thread or strongly contrasting thread can be used.

Finish off the stocking mouth with a strip of ribbon sewn to the inside and stitch a curtain ring at the back of the stocking to hang it.

**48.** *Draw these patterns up to a scale of 1 square to 1 inch to make stockings 14 inches deep* ▼

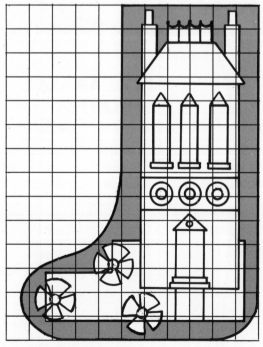

one square=1in

# Cinderella finger puppets

To make these finger puppets you will need only remnants of felt and an assortment of decorative trims – bits of lace, ric rac braid, ends of ribbon, small buttons, sequins – and some fabric adhesive.

To make the puppets make a cardboard template for each shape and use them to cut out the felt.

A template helps to achieve a good outline, particularly for circular shapes. The round shape is the head of the puppet and the other is for the body. Cut two round shapes and two bodies for each puppet. Machine stitch the two body pieces together along the two long sides, working on the right side. You can sew them together by hand using stab stitches if you prefer. Stitch along the two dotted lines indicated on the diagram to make a socket for the finger. This may have to be made even narrower for a small child's hand – take a measurement before stitching. The overall depth of the puppet may have to be cut down too.

Place the two head circles together, sandwiching a very small amount of cotton wool between them for slight padding. Paste all round the edge and slip the upper short edge of the body section between the circles. Stitch all round the edge of the circle, securing the body section as you stitch.

Cut features and other trims and glue or stitch them on.

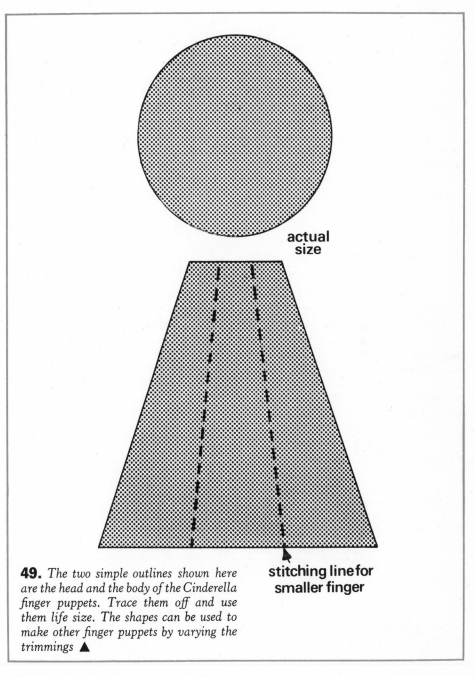

actual size

stitching line for smaller finger

**49.** *The two simple outlines shown here are the head and the body of the Cinderella finger puppets. Trace them off and use them life size. The shapes can be used to make other finger puppets by varying the trimmings* ▲

# String and paper zoo animals

Make a whole zoo of animals from newspaper and coloured twine. Basically, the animals are constructed from rolled up newspaper, secured into shape with Sellotape.

The method for making all kinds of animals is the same as given here.

### Making the giraffe

Roll a large double sheet of newspaper to make a tube about 1 inch in diameter. Secure the tube with pieces of Sello-tape. Bend one end about 1½ inches along for the head. Tape. Make another bend at the end of a long neck. Tape to secure. Cut into the tube with scissors to make the two back legs. Tape into shape. Cut off any excess paper. Roll half a sheet for the front legs, endeavouring to get the thickness of the tube the same as the back legs. Fold the tube in the middle and tape the two legs thus made to the main body. Cut the tubes to the correct length for front legs. Start covering the paper with twine beginning at the nose. Cut a small piece of felt and hold it over the nose section. Begin to wind the twine over the felt. When three or four strands are in position, tuck the end of the twine in and glue it under the strands. Wind the twine slowly and carefully to achieve absolute evenness. Wherever the twine seems inclined to slip out of alignment, such as under the front legs, smear a little adhesive on the paper and wind the twine onto it. Wind the legs separately from the body and tuck in and glue the twine ends. Make a tail from felt. Eyes are made from small beads on a patch of felt.

# Cork snake

**Here is an amusing toy to make from a few corks, a length of elastic and some paints. Use a piece of twine if elastic isn't available.**

Materials you will need:
Corks (11 were used for the snake illustrated)
Enamel paint, yellow and green
Red felt
18 inches of ¼ inch wide elastic or tape
Beads for eyes
Sharp knife

▼*Cut the corks into shape*

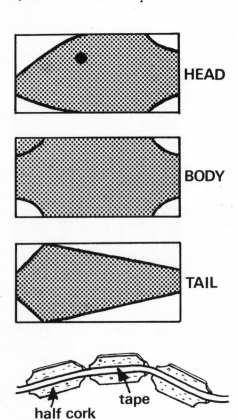

HEAD

BODY

TAIL

half cork    tape

▲*Assembling the snake*

Cut one cork for the tail as shown in the diagram. Cut the head cork. Cut each of the body corks as shown.
Cut all the body corks in half lengthwise. Cut a slit in the neck end of the head cork. Cut a slit in the flat end of the tail cork.
Glue the tape or elastic to one flat inner side of all the corks leaving a ¼ inch space between each cork.

When quite dry, glue the other half of each cork in position.
Slip a small elastic band round each cork to hold it during drying if necessary. Smear adhesive on one end of the tape and push it into the head cork with the tip of a knife. Smear adhesive on the other end and push it into the tail section. Paint the body green and yellow. Cut a small felt tongue and glue it to the head under the chin. Glue beads for eyes or paint them on if you prefer.

# Dragon marionette

**A marvellous dragon puppet to make based on a pair of wooden spoons and fabric scraps.**

Materials you will need:
2 identical wooden spoons
Springs from 4 1 inch diameter hair rollers
Lead dress or fishing weights
Packet of pipe cleaners, green if possible or colour them
Thin card
Metallic ricrac, gold paper, sequin, braid etc., to decorate
2 yellow marbles for eyes
Red felt, 13 inches by 2 inches
Button thread
Green and red Lurex fabric
Undercoat and enamel paint, red and green
15 inch strip 1 inch by 3 inch wood
3 screws for control
Impact adhesive

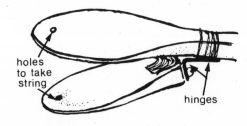

holes to take string

hinges

1. *The lower spoon head hinged to the upper*

### To prepare the head and body
Drill four holes in the handle of one of the spoons at 2 inch, 12 inches, 7 inches and 8 inches from the tip of the handle. These holes support the legs and must

be drilled from side to side of the handle, parallel with the bowl of the spoon. Paint the spoon bowls with undercoat, Leave the handles unpainted. When the undercoat is dry paint the bowl of each spoon red and the back green.
Cut off the unbored handle just below the bowl of the spoon. Discard this handle, retaining the bowl part for the dragon's lower jaw. To join the two jaws, glue one end of a 2 inch by 5 inch strip of felt to the sawn-off edge and anchor it down firmly with a small wood screw. Place the two spoon bowls together with the bowls facing and stick the other end of the felt to the handle of the upper spoon just below the bowl. Wind thread round the glued felt to hold it in place. Stick another strip of felt to the inside of the bowl to strengthen the first hinge (Fig. 1). Drill a small hole through the upper spoon bowl near the lip and a corresponding hole through the lower bowl. These holes will take the string which controls the creature's mouth.
Make the eyes next. Wind a 2 inch wide strip of red felt into a cone shape and use impact adhesive to stick a yellow marble inside it. Place the red felt cone inside a slightly larger cone of gold paper. Make another eye in the same way, and stick the eyes to the top of the upper jaw. Cut two strips of green lurex fabric and stick one over the top of each eye for a wrinkled eyelid.
The nostrils are two small circles of red felt and lengths of silver ricrac are glued to the inside of the top and bottom jaws to simulate teeth. Make a forked tongue by rolling a strip of red Lurex fabric round two pipe cleaners. Stick it inside the lower jaw, and protruding a little in front, as shown in the illustration.
To make the body bind the handle of the spoon firmly with a strip of green Lurex fabric, covering the rounded end of the handle.

### Making the legs
The dragon's legs are made from the wire hair rollers. Take the covering from each wire hair-roller spring and pull the coils apart a little to make them more springy. Bend the springs over into a curve. Cut off the last two or three coils from each spring to shorten them a little, and thread one or two lead weights onto the cut ends, securing the weights by bending over the spring ends.
Make four tubes of green Lurex fabric

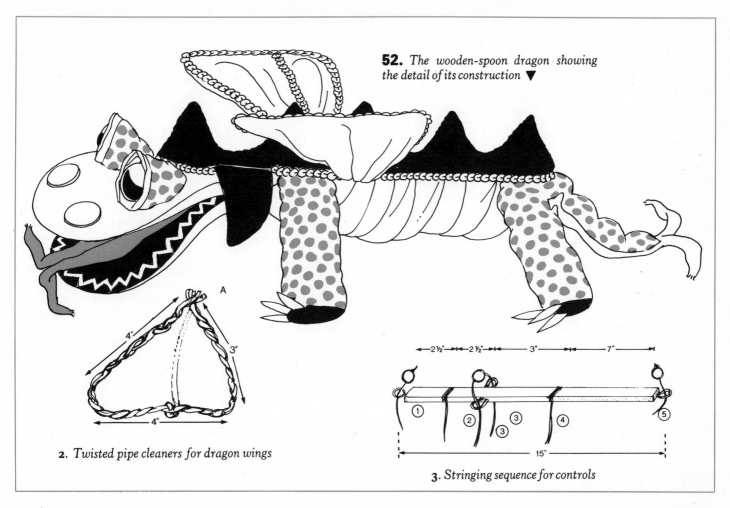

**52.** *The wooden-spoon dragon showing
the detail of its construction* ▼

**2.** *Twisted pipe cleaners for dragon wings*

**3.** *Stringing sequence for controls*

to cover the springs, tuck the raw edges inside the unweighted ends and oversew them to the wire. Oversew a circle of red felt to the raw edges of the tube on each weighted end, for the paw pads. Sew the legs firmly in pairs to the body through the drilled holes, passing the thread round the top ring of each spring.

### Underbody
Pad the underneath of the spoon handle between the legs with kapok and secure it with thread. Cut a strip of red Lurex fabric and wind it round the padding to give the effect of a paunchy stomach.

### Wings
Take two pipe cleaners and twist the ends together for about 1 inch. Do the same twice more with four more cleaners. Twist the three doubled lengths of pipe cleaner together, then bend them into the wing shape shown in Fig. 2. Reinforce with another pipe cleaner placed down the centre as shown, for a rib. Make another wing in the same way. Cover both wings with Lurex fabric, green on the upper side, red on the under, gathering the fabric at the point marked A. Sew the wings to either side of the dragon's back, about 1 inch behind the front legs, using the gathers at

A to form hinges so that the wings can be flapped up and down. Decorate the wing edges with sequin strip.

### Tail
Cut a piece of red Lurex fabric 2 inches wide and 6 inches long. Taper to a point on both sides to make an elongated triangular shape. Cut a similar shape in green Lurex fabric. With right sides facing, sew the sides of the triangles together. Turn to the side. Slip a weight into the pointed end and lightly stuff the rest of the tail. Work four rows of running stitches 1 inch apart across the width of the tail and draw up slightly to give the effect of a ridged reptilian tail. Sew the tail to the tip of the spoon handle. Make a forked tip for the tail end from red felt.

### Back spine
Take a strip of card 11 inches by 12 inches deep and cut one long side into 5 curved spikes. Cover each side of the card with red felt, allowing a 1 inch surplus along the straight edge. Sew the felt edges together along the curves. Work a line of running stitches along the straight edge close to the card. Open out the 1 inch surplus pieces and pin them along the centre of the dragon's back; the spine should start at a point

between the eyes. Stitch down the edges of the felt and card spine. Stick sequin strip on either side of the spine to cover the stitches. Cut two curved flaps of red felt and stick one on either side of the head to hide the join between the lower and upper jaws.

### Control
Insert a screw eye into each end of the 15 inch strip of wood, and one into each side of the wood 5 inches from one end. Following Fig. 3, take a length of thread from the holes in the jaw through one end hook (string 1). Tie a small bead on the end underneath the jaw and a large bead on the hook end so that it can be easily operated. Take string 2 from a point on the back spine just behind the head; a continuous string 3, with a bead in the centre so that it can be easily picked up, from each wing tip through a pair of screw eyes in the wood strip, adjusting the length so that the wings are slightly lifted. Run string 4 from the end of the spoon handle and tie it round the control; run string 5 from the tip of the tail through the second end hook with a bead at the hook end. Make nicks in the wood for all the strings and wind the string round, securing with a dab of glue.

## Paper plate faces

Paper plate faces are fun for children to do and make a good party project, prizes being awarded for the most original face. Supply children with poster paints, crayons, scraps of felt and knitting wool, pieces of coloured paper and some paste and leave them to it. If holes are cut for the eyes, the plates can be turned into masks, by tying a length of twine through holes made each side of the plate.

Paper plate faces make delightful wall decorations for a child's room and give him a chance to show off his artwork. Glue a short length of twine to the back of the plate so that it can be hung up.

## Fill the room with flags

In almost every part of the world, flags are used for decorations on feast days and for celebrations. In South America, children make their own paper flags.

Flags made of coloured tissue paper make a pretty room decoration and look wonderful for outdoor parties too. They're simple to do and make a good pre-party project when you want the children to sit quietly for a while. Because the failure rate is very low, even the smallest child could manage to make a flag all by himself.

These flags require only the very simplest folding to make the cut out patterns and no two flags seem to come out exactly alike. Coloured tissue paper works best because the colours are bright and clear and the flags flutter in an air current, but gift wrapping paper works almost as well. Cut a 30 inches by 20 inches sheet into eight pieces, each 10 inches by $7\frac{1}{2}$ inches. Take a piece and fold it in half. Cut shapes out on the fold. Open the flag and fold it the other way and cut out more shapes. Fold it diagonally and cut again. Every time you fold and cut you add to the pattern. The sides of the flag can be pinked, scalloped or fringed.

Mount the cut-out flags over uncut sheets of tissue for interesting two-coloured effects.

To mount the flags for hanging, coat an ordinary drinking straw with adhesive and roll the top edge of the flag onto the straw. Thread thin twine through the straws to make a garland.

### Tissue table mats and traymats

Unusual and pretty placemats for a party table can be made with cut-out tissue pasted over coloured cartridge paper. Make mats 15 inches wide by 10 inches deep. One effect is obtained by cutting the cartridge paper larger than the tissue mat so that the mat is framed in a solid colour border. A quite different look is achieved by cutting the tissue larger and fringing the edge.

## Dressing-up bags

Big brown paper bags, the kind supplied by grocery shops and bulk buying stores can be turned into dressing-up bags. The bags usually have a gusset and are made strongly enough to withstand the stresses of child's play.

Children generally hate putting their heads into the dark interior of a bag so cut the back open from top to bottom and stitch tie tapes to fasten. Cut good sized holes for arms and a large peephole in the front.

Animal and bird characteristics are either painted on using poster colours or cut from thin coloured poster paper.

▼ **54.** *Try out these folds and cut-outs and then invent some of your own*

▼ *To occupy a young invalid, let him cut up tissue paper mats for his trays*

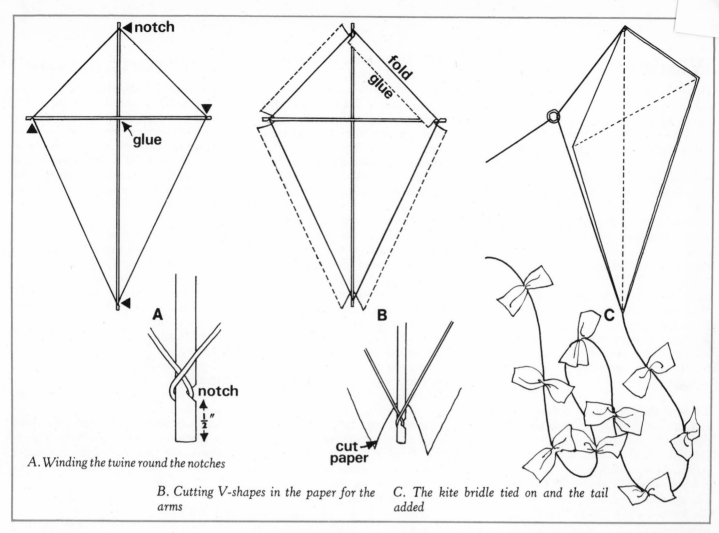

A. Winding the twine round the notches

B. Cutting V-shapes in the paper for the arms

C. The kite bridle tied on and the tail added

# A kite that really flies

This high-flier is one of the simplest of kite shapes to make but you must be careful with measurements because the proportions are important. The length must always be $\frac{1}{3}$ more than the width. The kite can be as large as 36 inches long and 24 inches wide or as small as 15 inches long and 10 inches wide.

Brightly coloured tissue paper was used for the kites illustrated but gift paper looks just as gay and ordinary newspaper makes an effective kite material too. Join large double sheets to make really big kites.

Materials you will need to make a kite 27 inches long by 18 inches wide:
Two large sheets of paper 30 inches by 20 inches

Two lengths of $\frac{1}{4}$" by $\frac{1}{4}$" wood, one 27 inches long and the other 18 inches long
Wood adhesive
Paper adhesive
Ball of thin strong twine
Sharp knife
Scissors
Curtain ring, 1 inch diameter

Mark the centre of the short length of wood. Make a mark 9 inches from one end of the longer piece of wood. With a sharp knife, cut a half-depth housing on both pieces of wood, exactly on the marks. Fit the two pieces of wood into a cross and glue. Place a weight on top of the join while it dries. Cut v-shaped notches on each arm of the cross, $\frac{1}{2}$ inch from the ends and on the side of the woodstick shown in the diagram. These notches are used to hold the twine frame.

Tie the twine round the notch in the bottom arm. Take the twine to the right arm and knot once, then take it to the top arm, knot once, to the left arm and knot once and back to the bottom arm, tying the end to the original knot. Place the strung kite down on one sheet of paper. Put a weight on the

centre of the cross to hold it down. Draw round the outline of the kite 1 inch from the string. Cut the shape out. Place the kite down on the paper again and cut v-shapes about 1 inch deep where the arms lie. Fold and glue the paper over the string all round. Leave to dry. Place the kite, wood side down on the second sheet of paper and draw round the outline. Cut out the shape and glue to the reverse of the kite, matching edges exactly.

Decorate with paper shapes if desired.

### Making the bridle

Cut a length of twine the length of the kite plus $\frac{1}{3}$ (36 inches for this kite).
Tie the curtain ring onto the twine about $\frac{1}{3}$ of the way along. Knot the bridle to the top and to the bottom arms of the kite. Drip adhesive onto the knots to make them secure.
Make a tail about 12 foot long by tying bows of paper to a length of twine. Tie to the bottom arm.
Tie the end of the ball of twine to the curtain ring.
And you're ready to fly!
(Bigger kites will need a longer tail by the way, or they won't fly as well).

# Windtoy

To make a windmill you will need either coloured paper, foil paper or pieces of acetate film. To make the windmill illustrated, two different kinds of paper are required.

Materials you will need:
Two different types of paper, a piece of each 5½ inches square
12 inch length of ¼ inch by ¼ inch wood or a garden cane
1 2-inch panel pin
1 large wooden bead
1 small bead. (The hole in both beads should be large enough for the panel pin to go through and yet not slip off.)
Sharp knife
Scrap of contrast paper
Sharp, pointed scissors
Bradawl and a hammer

Trace off the shape given in the diagram and cut out the shape from each of the different types of paper.
Cut out the five small holes with the points of the scissors.
Fit one windmill shape on the other exactly matching them and then slip the top one clockwise so that the con-

vex curve fits into the concave curve of the windmill below. They will lock together. Slip both shapes onto a spare panel pin, still locked together. Take each one of the windmill arms in turn and slip the hole onto the panel pin. You will be picking up arms of each of the windmills alternately if the two shapes are locked together properly. Leave the windmill aside.

Draw and cut out a circle of paper about 1½ inches diameter and pink the edges. Cut a hole in the centre. Put on one side and work on the stick. Make a hole in the wooden stick about 1 inch from one end. Don't make the hole right through, just enough to be able to push the panel pin in easily.

Thread the small bead onto the panel pin and push it against the pin head. Put the pinked circle on next facing towards the pin head. Now pick up the windmill and slip the whole thing off the panel pin and position it on the pin you are holding, facing towards the head. Put the large bead on last and then push the panel pin into the wooden stick. It may need a light tap to secure it. Make sure that there is enough clearance for the windmill to turn easily when you blow upon the vanes.

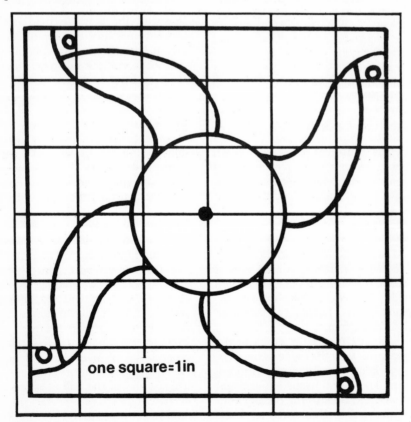

**57.** *Graph pattern for the windmill.* 1 *square* = 1 *inch*

# Paper party hats

**Paper party hats are fun to make and providing there is some adult supervision, children are quite good at making some styles themselves and get quite carried away with the decorative effects! A whole wardrobe of different styles can be made from the three basic shapes given, a cone, a pill box and a brim.**

Materials you will need:
Crêpe paper or gift wrapping paper
White cartridge paper or lightweight card from large food boxes
Scraps of sticky-backed paper for decoration (or shapes cut from the pages of coloured glossy magazines
Gold foil paper
Scissors
All-purpose adhesive
Sellotape
(Crêpe paper works best for hats because it doesn't tear easily and sews and glues well. All the hats illustrated are made on a stiff paper base. This is because the base makes the hat easier to work on and gives the hat a longer life.)

### Clown's hat
Measure a child's head—it is approximately 22 inches in circumference at about 10 years old. Make a cone, out of cartridge paper adding 1 inch to the measurement to overlap. Join the long sides with Sellotape. Cut out the cone shape again in crêpe paper and add ½ inch to the bottom curve. Cover the paper cone, overlapping the long sides and glueing them. Turn under the ½ inch at the bottom to the inside of the hat and glue down. To make the plume, cut a piece of crêpe paper 20 inches long by 10 inches deep. Roll it up and secure with tape. Cut down into the roll from one end about 7 inches. Shake out the plume. Glue the roll into the top of the clown's hat. Cut out a gold crescent and stick on the front.

### Witch's hat
Make a paper cone in the same way as for the clown's hat, and snip all round the lower edge with scissors, making ½ inch cuts about ½ inch apart. Fold the tabs back to the outside of the cone. Place the cone on a large piece of paper and draw round the cone with the tabs folded back out of the way. If the circle looks a bit uneven, place a suitably sized plate on the paper and

draw around that. Draw another circle outside of this, about 3 inches away. This is the brim. Cut the shape out. Cover the cone with crêpe paper.

Cover the upper brim with crêpe paper. Place the brim section over the cone so that the tabs lie against the under brim. Glue the tabs to the brim. Cover the under brim with crêpe paper and trim the brim edge with scissors to neaten. Cut a strip of crêpe paper for a hat band and glue round the base of the crown. Cut out suitable magic motifs and glue them to the front.

For a hallowe'en witch's hat, glue lengths of string or yarn to the inside of the hat band for hair.

## Pill box

Cut a strip of cartridge paper to the measurement of the child's head (about 22 inches), plus 1 inch for joining by $3\frac{1}{2}$ inches deep. Form the strip into a ring and join the short edges with tape. Place the ring on a large sheet of paper and draw round it with a felt pen. Remove the paper ring and draw round the circle again $\frac{1}{2}$ inch away. Snip into this edge making $\frac{1}{2}$ inch deep cuts about $\frac{1}{2}$ inch apart.
Fold the tabs inwards.
Cut a circle of crêpe paper to the dimensions of the circle without the tabs. Glue the crêpe paper to the circle with small dabs of adhesive. This is the crown of the pillbox. Place the crown on the table and fit the paper ring over it. Glue the tabs to the inside of the ring.
Cut a strip of crêpe paper to the measurements of the long strip, plus 1 inch more on the depth.
Turn a narrow hem on one long edge to neaten and glue down. Cover the ring with the crêpe paper, overlapping the join and glueing down; the neatened edge matches the edge of the crown.
Turn the other raw edge to the inside of the hat and glue down. Snip into it to make it lie smoothly.
**To make the cockade:** Cut a strip of contrasting crêpe paper as for the plume but curl the cut ends by pulling them gently over the blade of a knife with the ball of the thumb.

## Fez

Make the basic cone shape and cut off the point about 6 inches down. Place the cone, cut end down, on a sheet of paper to plan the crown. Cut a circle for the crown and add an

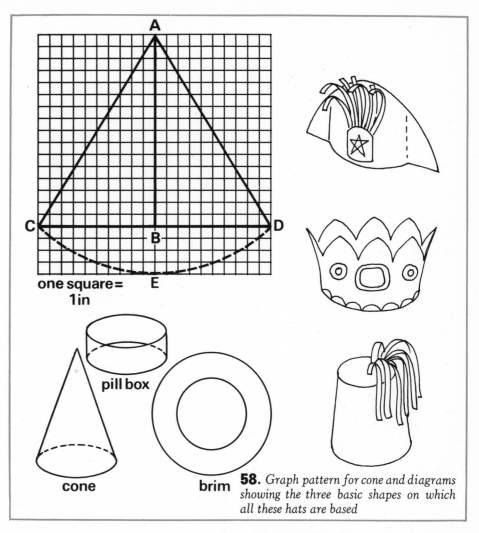

**58.** *Graph pattern for cone and diagrams showing the three basic shapes on which all these hats are based*

allowance for the tabs. Make up the crown as for the pill box. Make a plume for the top of the fez. Make a hole in the top of the fez for the plume.

## King's crown

Make a crown by cutting a strip of gold foil paper to the measurement of the child's head plus 1 inch for joining. Cut one edge into points or, using a cup, draw and cut scallops. Cut coloured paper shapes for jewels. Line the crown with a strip of cartridge paper if it seems to flop a bit.

## Pirate's hat

Cut a circle of coloured cartridge paper about 30 inches diameter. Fold in half and cut along the fold. Place the two halves together and mark the centre of the straight edges. Measure $5\frac{1}{2}$ inches to left and right of the centre mark. Draw a pencil line to the top of the hat from both these marks. Glue the two halves of the hat together, smearing adhesive only on the two segments outside the pencil line. Cut a skull and crossbones from white paper and glue to the front. This shape will also make a Napoleon hat with the addition of a cockade.

## Flowered hat

A great favourite with little girls and simpler to make than it looks.

Make the crown first. Cut a piece of crêpe paper to the measurement of the child's head plus 1 inch for joining and 3 inches deep.

Seam the short sides by sewing it with running stitches. Gather up one long edge to about 4 inches and keep the gathers on the thread. Cut two circles of crêpe paper about $2\frac{1}{2}$ inches in diameter and glue the circles to both sides of the gathering. Cut tabs all round the lower edge of the crown. Cut a brim as for the witch's hat and cover the upper side of the brim with crêpe paper. Slip over the crown section and glue the tabs in position.

Cover the underside of the brim with crêpe paper and trim the edge of the brim with scissors.

Make a hat band by cutting a strip of crêpe paper and folding it once. Fish-tail the ends. Make paper flowers by cutting 12 inch by 3 inch strips of crêpe paper, folding them once along the length and winding them into flower heads. Glue to secure the ends and then glue them to the hat.

# Christmas window

In Scandinavia, some families decorate windows with cut-out snowflakes, seasonal motifs and snow scenes, made of coloured papers and foils. The windows look pretty from both inside and outside, particularly when the shapes are cut in transparent materials. Make the Nativity Christmas window in coloured tissue paper which will give a charming stained glass effect. The diagram gives a shape for a tree, a figure which can be adapted to make the Wise men, the Shepherds and the Holy Family, a sheep, a crown, a hat and the Christ Child. Draw the shapes on to stiff paper, cut out, and then cut the tissue paper out round the outline. Use a clear adhesive for glueing the shapes onto the glass and overlap some of them for a striking effect. Warning! If a window is inclined to be covered in condensation, it is wiser to avoid this type of decoration.

# Party piece

A very simple table centrepiece to make for a children's party using a cardboard box and chocolate beans. The beans are pushed into a thin covering of icing sugar and can, of course, be taken off and eaten.
If the house is for decoration only, spread Gesso, mixed fairly stiffly, over the cardboard and push the sweets into the surface before it dries. A sprinkling of glitter powder will give the decorations a Christmas look. To make the house structure, cut the gables from the box flaps at each end. Cut the roof from another box, with a hole for the chimney stack. Insert a small box in the roof hole, securing it with Sellotape. Make a chimney with a small tube of paper. Cut windows with shutters on the sides; cut the door to stand open at one end and cut holes for gable windows.
Use scraps of coloured paper for the window panes. We used red cellophane for our house, but any transparent or semi-opaque paper would do. Cut and stick on the inside for a neat finish.

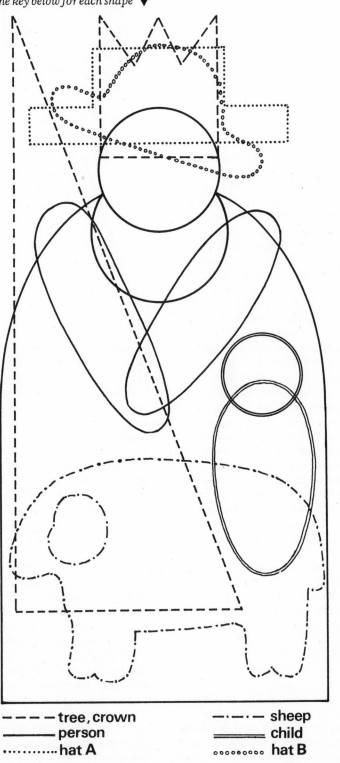

**59.** *Here are the seven shapes which make up the Nativity window; a tree which is cut out on the fold; a figure, to adapt for the three Wise Men, the Shepherds, Joseph and Mary; the Christ Child in swaddling clothes and a sheep. Three different kinds of headwear are given. Follow the lines shown in the key below for each shape* ▼

- – – – tree, crown
——— person
• • • • • • hat A
- · – · – sheep
═══ child
∘∘∘∘∘∘∘ hat B

# Papier mâché

Papier mâché is a fascinating craft and can be a most inexpensive way of making toys and gifts for children. Because it is so easy to do, adults can produce quite professional looking results at their first attempt while children, who take to papier mâché like ducks to water, find the craft an enormously satisfying outlet for their creativity. Only four basic materials are needed; newspaper, white plain flour, water and table salt. The salt is added to the mixture to preserve the paste during drying.

Basically, there are two kinds of papier mâché and both have been used to make toys in this section. The first is a layering technique and involves tearing newspaper into strips, covering the strips with paste and applying them in layers to the surface of a mould. In the second method, the newspaper is torn up, soaked in water for a long time, squeezed out and then mixed with flour and water paste to make a plastic pulp which can be used for modelling. The savings pigs, the masks and the tumbler dolls are made using the layering method while the farmyard and the battlefield use both the layering method and papier mâché pulp.

## Making the paste

Ingredients:
White plain flour
Table salt
Cold water
Boiling water

Any quantity of paste can be mixed and for each quart of paste, 1 tablespoon of salt is added.
Put the flour and salt into a bowl and add cold water gradually, stirring all the time to prevent lumps forming. Add sufficient cold water to produce a mixture the consistency of thick cream. Add boiling water to the mixture, stirring all the time. The paste will thicken and become slightly translucent. The consistency of the finished paste should be smooth and rather thick. The salt will preserve the paste during drying but if you are working on a project for several days it is advisable to store the bowl of paste in the refrigerator between work sessions. This way, it will keep fresh for about a week.

## The layering method

Tear, never cut, newspaper into strips or pieces. It isn't advisable to use the glossy paper from magazines because this kind of paper doesn't absorb paste very well.

The torn strips will vary in size and shape depending on what you are making. The masks used strips approximately 5 inches by 1 inch while the savings pigs and tumbler dolls used quite small pieces – approximately 1 inch square for the large pig and $\frac{1}{2}$ inch square for the smaller pig and the dolls. Cover the strips of paper with paste on both sides. If you hate to get your fingers sticky, use a brush. Otherwise, dip the strips in the paste and remove the excess paste with the forefinger and thumb of the other hand. Apply the pasted strips to the surface of the mould, slightly overlapping the pieces of paper and arranging them at different angles. Cover the entire surface. Leave each layer to dry before applying the next.

If you are covering a mould which is to be kept as part of the finished structure, such as the cardboard box which forms the farm house, only three layers of papier mâché will be needed. If the mould is going to be removed, such as the balloon used for the savings pig, eight or nine layers will have to be done.

The exception is the kind of make which isn't going to receive a great deal of stress in use, such as a gift egg. Working over a mould such as an orange, only four layers would be needed.

# Masks

The masks are made on balloon moulds and are easy enough for children to make for themselves. Inflate the balloon to approximately the size of the child's head. Place the balloon in a bowl of about the same size so that half of the balloon is above the bowl's rim. For the nose, cut and fix a segment of an egg carton to the surface of the balloon with Sellotape before oiling. Oil all over the area of the balloon to be covered and proceed to apply pasted strips. The strips can be as big as 5 inches by about 1 inch for a mask so that coverage is quick.

Cover the nose section in with the rest of the face and build up eyebrows with thicker layers of paper. Three layers are sufficient for a mask. When the paper is quite dry throughout, remove the mask from the balloon – it comes away quite easily – and trim the edge with scissors. Cut holes for the eyes and mouth and pierce two small holes each side of the head. Paint the features with poster colours. No varnishing is necessary. Thread elastic through the holes to fasten round the head.

Make animal masks using the same method and use food boxes for the noses – cut them down in shape if necessary – and use half of an egg carton segment for ears. Beaks for bird masks are made over a four inch long cone.

▲ *Stick the segment of egg carton down onto the balloon with tape and build up three layers of pasted strips*

# Savings pigs

**The large pig was made over a rubber balloon and the smaller pig was made on a lemon.**

Materials you will need:
Quantity of newspaper
Flour and water paste
Vegetable oil
Soft white paper, such as tissue handkerchiefs or toilet paper
Balloon (for supporting a large pig)
Lemon (for supporting a small pig)
Basin (for a large pig)
Egg cup (for a small pig)
1 inch curtain ring
Felt scraps
Modeller's paints or poster paints
Paintbrush
Sharp, pointed knife
Decorative transfers
Pliers

### Making the body

Inflate the balloon to about 5 inches diameter and knot securely. Coat the balloon with oil, using the hands. Oil the lemon in a similar way. Oiling the mould makes it easier to remove it from the dried papier mâché. You'll find it easier to work if the balloon and the lemon are supported on a container. Use the basin for the balloon and an egg cup for the lemon. Keep the tied end of the balloon as the tail end of the pig.
Cover the entire surface of the oiled mould with pieces of pasted paper and leave to dry.

### Making legs and snout

When two or three layers have been applied and have dried out, add the pig's legs.

Tear strips of paper about 5 inches long by 1 inch (for the large pig) or 2 inches by $\frac{3}{4}$ inch (for the smaller pig). Paste the strips and roll them up to make a solid shape about $\frac{1}{2}$ inch diameter. Soften one end by tearing the paper slightly. Balance the leg on the surface of the balloon body and hold it in position with pieces of Sellotape.
Tear more long, narrow strips and paste them up the sides of the leg with about $\frac{1}{3}$ of the strip laying on the body. Two layers of strips all round the leg should hold it to the body securely. Make and fix three more legs in the same way. Let the legs dry before doing the snout.
The balloon body will have to be stood on its tail end in the basin to do the snout. Make the snout from pasted strips in exactly the same way as the legs except that the strips will be shallower—about $\frac{1}{2}$ inch deep. Make a disc about $1\frac{1}{4}$ inches diameter and $\frac{3}{4}$ inch thick for the larger pig. When the snout has been taped and paste-stripped into position, smooth out the join with a wetted finger tip and taper off the under-snout into the body.
If the pig is to have a nose ring, put it in now. Cut a segment from a curtain ring with a pair of pliers, open up the cut ends slightly and push the ends into the soft papier mâché. As the paper dries the ring will be held firm. Continue to cover the entire pig with layers of paper until there are at least eight.

### Finishing

When the pig is completely dry throughout, remove the mould. For the large pig you have only to pierce the balloon and pull it out of the body through the hole in the papier mâché. To remove the lemon from the smaller

▼ *Make Easter egg shells on an orange mould*

pig, cut through the papier mâché with a sharp knife, cutting round the width of the lemon. Remove the lemon (it's still edible!), and then glue the two halves of the pig together again.
The pigs now need a good painting surface and this is achieved by covering them with two layers of the soft, white paper. Tear the paper into very small pieces and paste them on, adding more pieces wherever the surface seems slightly uneven. Two layers will probably be sufficient if you have been applying the newspaper strips properly. The small pig may need three layers to hide the join across his middle.
When the finishing layers have dried out completely, cut a slit in the back for the coins to go through using a sharp, pointed knife.

### Painting and decorating

Paint the pig all over in a light-toned colour. Model maker's enamels are suitable. Alternatively, paint the pigs with poster colours, mixing the paint fairly thickly, and sealing the surface afterwards with two coats of clear varnish.
Transfer motifs are a quick way of achieving a professional-looking decoration but paint the decoration yourself for a more personal touch. A child would love her own name on her savings pig for instance or paint in a phrase such as 'save the pennies . . .' in a flower border for an older child. On an enamelled surface, paint the decorations in enamel paint but if the pig is painted with poster colours, water colour paints or felt tipped pens can be used for decorating. Paint dots for eyes. Apply the varnish after the colour is quite dry.
Cut felt ears and glue them on when the enamel or varnish has dried completely.

### More things to make

Other animals can be made in much the same way. A long balloon will make a sheep for instance. A section of an egg carton is taped on one end for the nose and short lengths of wool, curled tightly round a matchstick into curlicues, are glued all over the back and sides for fleece.
Two long balloons, taped together would make a giraffe and a large-sized balloon would form the mould for a sitting hen for an Easter table decoration.

▲ *A savings pig complete with legs and snout*

# Tumbler dolls

The tumbler dolls illustrated are made using blown eggs as moulds but if you feel nervous about egg blowing, blow them after the papier mâché coating has been applied and dried – you won't risk a disaster that way. Only two layers of newspaper strip papier mâché are necessary as the shells stay inside. Two layers of soft tissue paper are applied finally to give a smooth finish.

Poster colours are suitable for decorating the dolls as long as two coats of clear varnish are applied afterwards. The dolls illustrated are based on the traditional Russian dolls made of wood but yours could be painted to look like Humpty Dumpty or as clowns.

When the newspaper strips have dried and before applying the soft tissue finish, cut a small hole in the top of the egg and drip some adhesive into the bottom. Drop some lead shot onto the adhesive and leave to dry. Close the hole with pasted strips. The lead shot weights the doll so that when it is pushed over, it rolls upright again.

# Woodland models

A very good modelling material can be made from cornflour and salt – just the thing for those days when children want to make models – and haven't any clay. All the woodland models illustrated were made from the quantity of mixture given here. A ring of toadstools painted with spotted red caps would make a pretty table centre with a small bowl of flowers in the middle.

Ingredients:
1 cup table salt
1 cup cornflour or cornstarch
¾ cup of cold water

Put the cornflour and salt into a basin and stand the basin in a saucepan of hot water. Add the cold water gradually stirring all the while. Keep stirring as the saucepan of water boils and when the mixture has become so thick that you cannot stir, spoon the mixture onto a plate to cool. When the mixture

has become cold enough to handle, knead to make it quite smooth.

The mixture makes a perfect modelling medium for children and there is little likelihood that a very small child will eat it. It wouldn't do him any harm if he did – but it tastes so salty that he isn't likely to try.

The mixture dries quite hard overnight and with an attractive crystalline surface which takes poster colours well.

# Farmyard

**Papier mâché can be used to make marvellous play-plan models with the help of food boxes and scraps of cardboard. Houses, villages, castles, ports and islands are all possible projects.**

Materials you will need:
Piece of hardboard 2 ft by 2 ft
Wood battening
Food boxes
Corrugated cardboard

Thin cardboard
Newspaper
Papier mâché pulp
Flour and water paste
All-purpose adhesive
Long-handled brush for paste
Sharp knife
Scissors
White emulsion paint
Model maker's enamel paints or poster colours
Clear varnish and brush

The most important thing to remember is that the model must be made to the scale of the toy vehicles, vessels, animals and people which will be used. You will need quite a lot of papier mâché pulp so make sure there is sufficient ready for the job.

Besides the main farm house, the farmyard contains a pigsty, a cow barn and a hay barn. Beside the house is a lean-to where the woodpile is kept. The main buildings are made of food boxes cut down to scale and covered with two or three layers of papier mâché strips. Pulp has been used to model the walls, grass, bushes and farmyard furrows.

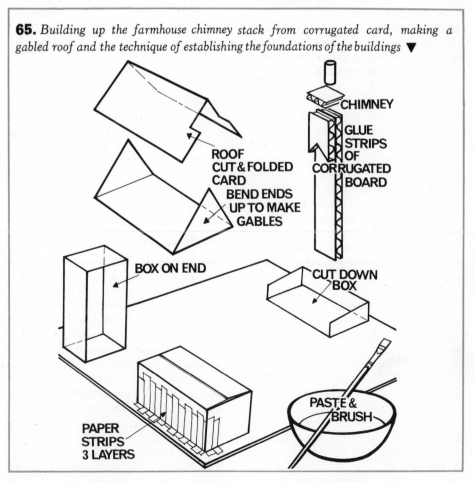

**65.** *Building up the farmhouse chimney stack from corrugated card, making a gabled roof and the technique of establishing the foundations of the buildings* ▼

ROOF CUT & FOLDED CARD

BEND ENDS UP TO MAKE GABLES

CHIMNEY
GLUE STRIPS OF CORRUGATED BOARD

BOX ON END

CUT DOWN BOX

PASTE & BRUSH

PAPER STRIPS 3 LAYERS

Fix battening to the underside of the hardboard on all the edges to strengthen the board and prevent cockling during drying. Cover the entire surface of the hardboard with strips of newspaper, pasting it down as you work. When the paper is dry, plan out the farmyard by arranging your selected food boxes where you think they might go. It is a good idea to have one or two toy animals and a human figure on hand to help the scale. Draw round the outline of the boxes with a felt tipped pen when you have them arranged to satisfaction.

Start with the main farmhouse building and glue the box to the floor of the farmyard. Tear strips of newspaper and paste them up the sides of the farmhouse walls, half on the walls, half on the ground. Build up at least three layers to secure the box to the hardboard. Glue down and secure the base of each of the farmhouse buildings in the same way.

Cut and fold roofs and structures such as the chimney stack from corrugated cardboard and glue them in position. Make the pigsty walls and the cow barn from pieces of corrugated card, taped together on the inside. Roofs are glued on. Make a pond from a circle of tin – the lid cut from a tin of coffee is about the right size.

When all the buildings have been erected, cover the entire surface of the farm yard and buildings with strips of pasted newspaper and leave to dry.

### Preparing the pulp

Now prepare the papier mâché pulp. Squeeze all the excess water out of the soaked newspaper and then mix the pulp with the flour and water paste. Knead the mixture until it is quite smooth. Mould the pulp to make the walls round the farmyard, bushes outside the farmhouse, grass round the duckpond and, if you have a toy tractor, run the tractor's wheels through pulp spread on the paths for an authentic farmyard look.

Leave the pulp to dry out thoroughly. This takes about a week.

Meanwhile, design and cut the doors and windows from thin cardboard. You can get ideas for styles and shapes from home furnishing magazines. Paint the doors and windows before sticking them on.

Give the entire farmyard and buildings a coat of white emulsion paint. Paint in realistic colours with poster colours and finish the model off with two coats of clear varnish.

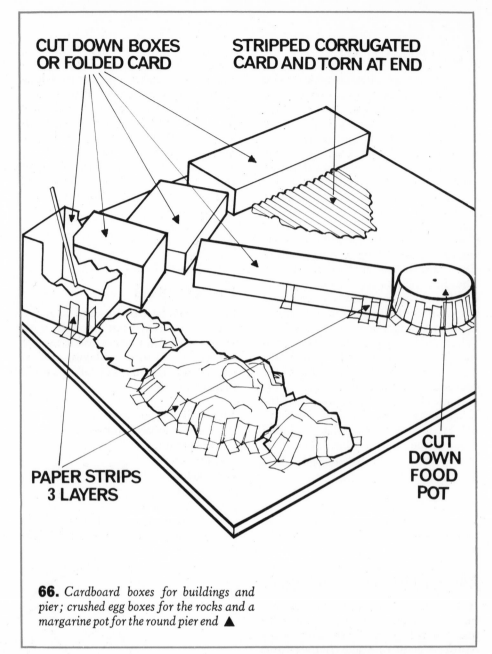

**CUT DOWN BOXES OR FOLDED CARD**

**STRIPPED CORRUGATED CARD AND TORN AT END**

**PAPER STRIPS 3 LAYERS**

**CUT DOWN FOOD POT**

**66.** *Cardboard boxes for buildings and pier; crushed egg boxes for the rocks and a margarine pot for the round pier end* ▲

# Battlefield

The battlefield is made in a similar way to the farm. Decide first which particular battle scene you are going to depict – and this will depend largely on the soldier collection which is going to be used with the battlefield. Historical battles are interesting to do and involve one in checking reference books to plan the terrain exactly.

The battlefield illustrated is modern and depicts a commando raid on a small fishing port – giving great scope for landing craft, vehicles and two different armies of soldiers.

Plan out the area on the prepared hard

wood base. The pier is a row of food boxes ending with a margarine pot. The rocks are heaped food boxes, glued together and covered with pulp. Tear or cut away part of the boxes being used for main buildings to indicate gun damage. Make steps, sheds, dug-outs, trenches and gun emplacements.

When you think you have planned sufficient structures for the soldiers and the area looks suitably blasted, mould hills, rocks, grass, beaches etc., with pulp. The sea ripples on the model illustrated are wisps of cotton wool soaked in paste. Smooth off those areas of the pulp which need it with a finger dipped in paste. Leave the model to dry out for at least a week.

Give a coat of white emulsion paint and finish off with poster colours and two coats of clear varnish.

# Tin can makes

Cans which are going to be turned into toys or models should be undamaged because it is almost impossible to bang out a dent. Remove the label by soaking the can in warm water and dry the can thoroughly. Almost all tin can toys look better for a coat of paint so give the can a coat of white emulsion ready for the finishing paint job with enamel.

## Pop-up puppet

A simple toy which will amuse a baby for as long as you 'pop' it. Animal pop-ups are made on the same principle.

Materials you will need:
1 beer can
Length of dowelling 20 inches long
Wooden ball or a pingpong ball
7 inches twine
Small balls or large beads for the hands
Scraps of fabric for clothes

Remove the top of the can and make a hole in the bottom large enough to take the dowelling. Drill a hole in the wooden ball and fit it to the top of the stick. Tie the twine to the stick about ½ inch below the ball. This is for the arms and is clearly illustrated in the diagram.
Make the clothes and dress the puppet. The dress should be the same length and the same width as the can. Gather the neck of the dress round the puppet's neck and glue in place. Cover the can with the same fabric as that used for the doll's dress. Tie the little balls or beads to the ends of the arms (which is the twine passing through the dress sleeves). Paint a happy face on the ball and make hair with scraps of fabric or knitting wool. Make a cone-shaped hat of paper and fabric and glue it to the top of the head. If the end of the stick is pulled the puppet disappears. Push the stick up and out pops the puppet.

## Painted pencil tins

Another bright idea with tins and cans. Paint the outsides or cover them with coloured paper. Decorate with cut-out motifs, initials, names and shapes. Use the cans as practical yet pretty containers for pencils and pens. Glue two or three small tins of different heights together for an unusual desk set.

## Tin can tanker truck

Once you have made this professional-looking tin toy vehicle, other ideas for trucks, cars and trains will occur to you and you'll look twice at every can about to be thrown out. The truck illustrated has rings cut from plastic reels for economy but suitable wheels can be purchased from model makers shops.

Materials you will need:
1 pint oil can
2 corned beef cans
Piece of ½ inch wood, 8½ inches long by 3½ inches wide
4 plastic reels or spools
2 buttons
3 big-headed nails
Nuts and washers
Sellotape
Strong all purpose adhesive
Enamel paints
Saw, hammer, bradawl

Tape one corned beef can to the side of the other, for the bonnet and cab. Saw the ends from the three spools to make six wheels. Fit the wheels to the wooden base as follows: – fit a washer onto the nail, then the wheel, next the nut and lastly another washer. Hammer the nail into the wood gently, and make sure that the wheels turn freely. Four wheels go at the rear of the vehicle, two each side and two at the front. Flatten the oil can on one side to enlarge the area of contact with the wooden base.
Glue the oil can and the corned beef cans to the wooden base and touching each other. Leave to dry.
Paint the vehicle with enamel colours. Cut one more wheel from the fourth spool and glue it to the top of the tank. A small cap from a tube finishes the tank off.
Two gilt plastic buttons are glued onto the front of the radiator for headlamps.

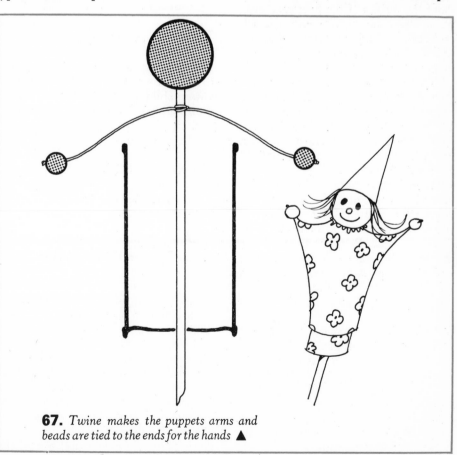

**67.** *Twine makes the puppets arms and beads are tied to the ends for the hands* ▲

# 70

## Indoor golf

Indoor golf is a wonderful indoor game for a rainy day and one that all the family can play. Make this attractive looking set from six beer cans.

Materials you will need:
Six beer cans
Stiff card
Matt black paint
Enamel paints, 6 colours
Rub-down numerals 1 to 6
2 24 inch lengths of $\frac{3}{8}$ inch dowelling
Two small pieces of plastic foam
Sharp knife
All purpose adhesive

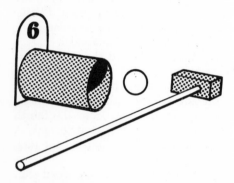

Paint the insides of the beer cans matt black. Paint the outsides with enamel, each can a different colour. Cut six pieces of card, $4\frac{3}{4}$ inches long by the diameter of the card. Cover the cards with white paper or paint them white. Round off one short end. Leave the other end square and glue each card to the bottom of a can, the straight edge level with the rim. Rub down a numeral on each one. Numbers can be cut from a calendar for economy.

Make the golf sticks as follows: Cut two 24 inch lengths of dowelling and paint them white. Cut two pieces of plastic foam, each $3\frac{1}{2}$ inches long by $1\frac{1}{2}$ inches wide. Paint them with black enamel. The foam will become quite stiff when the paint dries. When dry, cut a small hole in the top of each piece near one end and glue the stick in the hole.

Indoor golf can be played in a number of ways but the simplest is to arrange the numbered cans in a semi-circle on the far side of the room and putt the ball (a pingpong ball would do), into each of the cans in sequence. If the ball goes into a can and the number isn't in sequence, go back to the beginning and start again.

# 71

## Clucking hen

**It takes a little practice to produce the right noise but children usually manage to achieve it without too much trouble.**

Materials you will need:
1 tin can
Length of twine
Enamel paint and felt scraps if desired
Resin
Bradawl

Pierce a round hole in the bottom of the can. Paint the can at this stage and trim with felt to look like a hen's head if desired.
Thread about 30 inches of twine through the hole. Make a knot on the end inside the can. The can hangs supported on the knot. Rub resin down the string making sure every part of it is covered. Hold the other end of the twine and draw the first finger and thumb of the other hand down the string jerkily. A clucking noise will seem to come from the can.

# 72

## Tin can stilts

**Tin can stilts need very little practice to become an expert walker and quite young children get a lot of fun out of them. But don't let them attempt to walk up or down steps on them – this can be dangerous.**

Materials you will need for one pair of stilts:
Two cans of the same size
Strong twine
Can piercer
Emulsion paint
Enamel paint and transfers if desired

Make sure that the tops of the cans are cleanly cut. Give the cans a coat of white emulsion paint.
Turn a can on end (open end down), and with the can piercer (the kind that makes triangular holes), pierce holes on both sides of the can just below the rim and opposite each other. Pierce the second can in the same way. Paint the cans with enamel paint at this stage. Cut two lengths of twine – the length depends on the height and age of the

child but about 40 inches is usual. Thread the twine through both holes and tie a large knot inside the can.
To use the stilts, the child places a foot on each can and holding a loop of twine in each hand, walks. Tin can stilts are good for back-yard races.

# Old socks and stockings

It is hardly worth darning socks, stockings and tights these days because as they are mostly made of manmade fibres, holes appear only when the garment is becoming generally worn anyway. Odd socks and stockings can be cut into strips and crocheted on a large hook into chains. The lengths, sewn together in strips or rounds, make brightly coloured and long-lasting rugs.
Tights and stockings make good washable soft-toy stuffing too. Children will enjoy cutting them up into shreds on a rainy day.
Socks, stockings and tights can be made into puppets. With a little help with the seams and sewing, children can decorate the puppets themselves to make favourite television or story book characters.

# Hand puppet from a sock

An old pair of socks will make a hand puppet. It doesn't matter if there are holes. Cut the worn part away and sew up the seam.

### Poor Hottentot

Cut the welt off. From it cut two pieces each 2½ inches long and 1¼ inches wide for arms. Round off the short ends. On the wrong side, fold in half lengthwise, seam the long side and one short end. Put the sock on the hand and mark the place where the arms would feel most comfortable for the fingers to manipulate.

Cut a slit in each side, ½ inch long and seal the edges with nail varnish to prevent runs.

Stitch the arms to the sock on the wrong side.

Stuff the toe of the sock with cotton wool, a ball of wool or the other sock rolled up. Make a small tube of cardboard and smear it with glue. Push this into the head stuffing for a finger to fit into.

Tie the neck with a piece of black thread. Push three curtain rings onto the neck and hold in position with two or three stitches. Make a small necklace of beads and secure to the neck in the same way.

Stitch small curtain rings to each side of the head for earrings.

Make features in felt and glue in position.

Make a headband in felt. Glue two small feathers to the puppet's head and glue the headband over them.

Finish off the edges of the sock by sealing with nail polish and then making a narrow hem.

# Snake arm puppet

Arm puppets which use the fingers and thumb for opening the mouth are made from a long stocking or from one leg of a pair of tights. The inside of the mouth section will look more appealing cut out in felt, but there isn't any reason why this part shouldn't be cut from the welt of the stocking or the widest part of the tight's leg.

Arm puppets can, of course, be made from other fabrics too—felt is particularly good. Keep interesting scraps of trims on hand for decorating faces— buttons, beads, short lengths of wool, braid, ribbon etc.

Other creatures which make up well as arm puppets are lions with bushy black yarn manes, beagle dogs with floppy felt ears and an appealing expression, sea serpents, cats and all kinds of fish. Use the basic instructions given for the snake and adapt the design with felt ears, tongues, teeth, manes, scales, etc.

▼ *Trace-off pattern for the snake's inside mouth and the forked tongue*

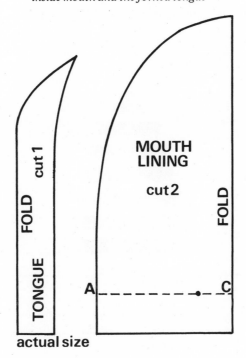

FOLD

TONGUE

cut 1

MOUTH LINING

cut 2

FOLD

A - - - - C

**actual size**

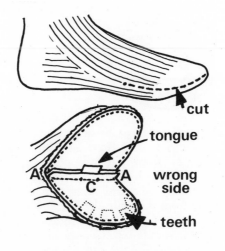

cut

tongue

A    C    A    **wrong side**

teeth

▲ *Cutting the sock and the technique for inserting the inside mouth*

Cut the foot of the stocking or tight's leg along the toe seam.

Elongate the cut 1½ inches further into the foot. Seal off the cut edges with clear nail varnish to prevent runs. Cut the inside mouth shape out twice. On the wrong side of the stocking, match the two felt shapes to the two cut edges and pin. Baste and stab stitch all round or machine stitch. Cut out the tongue in felt. Still working on the wrong side, insert the tongue shape into the stocking and pin the straight edged end of tongue between the straight edges of the inside mouth section. Stitch the edges together A-C-A, stitching through the tongue as well.

Turn the stocking to the right side and glue the eyes in position.

Cut the inside mouth shape out in stiff cardboard and insert this into the lower jaw of the puppet. This helps a child to operate the lower jaw with the thumb.

If the creature is to have teeth instead of a tongue, cut pieces of felt and pin and baste the teeth to the curved edge of one section of the inside mouth, with the teeth lying inwards and stitch the edge as before.

Paint the outline of the mouth with red paint and paint in two blue eyes with black pupils.

# Savings sock

Although a savings sock can be made from an odd, used sock for a gift, a new sock is rather nicer. Buy an inexpensive pair and make matching gifts for two children.

Measure the mouth of the sock and cut a circle of stiff card or hardboard to the diameter of the measurement.

Cut a hole for a mouth or a slit for the money to go through.

Mount the circle on a circle of felt, ¼ inch larger all round. Cut the slit or mouth though the felt also.

Pin and then stitch by hand, the felt to the mouth of the sock.

Finish off the seam by working chain stitch all round the join.

Either crochet a loop to hang the sock or glue a length of ribbon round the edge of the sock, making a loop from the two ends.

# 76

## Draughts (checkers) board

Accurate cutting of the paper is important if you want a really professional finish. Try making a chess set too—choose steel nuts, screws, bolts, wing nuts, washers etc., and screw them together to make suitable shapes.

Materials you will need:
24 bottle caps
Cardboard
Cellulose filler such as Polyfilla
Enamel Paints
Newspaper or magazine pages
Coloured shiny paper
Adhesive

Cut a piece of cardboard $17\frac{5}{8}$ inches square. Cut strips of the coloured paper to bind the edges, $1\frac{1}{2}$ inches wide. Take $\frac{3}{4}$ inch over to the back of the card and mitre the corners neatly.
Draw a pencil line $\frac{1}{8}$ inch inside the paper edging all round. Draw pencil lines across the card both ways 2 inches apart, dividing the card into 64 squares.
The board illustrated used typematter cut from the columns of a newspaper, and cut into 2 inch squares and glued down. If this effect is desired, make sure that all the type reads the same way up.
For a different effect, cut up the half toned photographs from glossy magazines for the black squares and use type matter for the lighter toned squares. Accurate cutting of the squares is very important.
After all the squares have been glued down and dried out, give the whole board at least three coats of clear varnish, letting each coat dry thoroughly before applying the next.

### To make the draughtsmen
Mix the filler and pour into the bottle caps. When dry, sandpaper the filler so that it is smooth and paint the cap with enamel on both sides. Choose two contrasting colours.

# 77

## Bottle top advent card

An unusual advent card to make as a pre-Christmas gift or for a child to make for himself, with a little adult help.

Materials you will need:
25 metal bottle caps
Heavy cardboard
Coloured paper
Felt, in three tones of green and a scrap of pink
Glass headed pins
Narrow baby ribbon or gift ribbon
Old Christmas cards or gift wrapping
Rub-down numerals
Poster colours or enamel paints
Varnish and a soft brush

▲ Use contrasting greens for the branches.
▼ Give the ribbon a twist before glueing it down

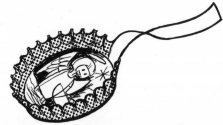

You will need 25 Christmas motifs and these can be cut from old Christmas cards or from gift wrapping paper. Some designs have holly leaves or little Christmas bells and these can be cut away from the main design. A Christmas issue of a magazine will have some suitable motifs too. Choose something very special for the cap numbered for Christmas day—the Holy Family for example. Prepare the bottle caps first.

Paint each one a different colour, but the silver and gold caps can be left if they don't carry printing on them. Paint the inside of the caps black.
If you are using poster colours and the paint doesn't flow on the metal, mix a little soap with the paint.
Cut the Christmas motifs into square shapes so that they just fit into the caps. You can cut circles if you prefer but accurate circles are rather more difficult to do.
Cut a piece of ribbon for each cap, about $1\frac{1}{4}$ inches long, and glue one end inside the cap. Glue the motif over the ribbon.
Cut a piece of card 12 inches square. Cut a piece of coloured paper 13 inches square and cover the card, taking the paper to the wrong side neatly and mitring the corners. Glue down the edges.
Cut $1\frac{1}{8}$ inch strips of green felt to the following lengths: $5\frac{1}{2}$ inches, $6\frac{1}{2}$ inches, 8 inches, 9 inches, $10\frac{1}{2}$ inches and 11 inches. Round off one corner at both ends. Cut a triangle of green felt for the top of the tree and a square of pink felt for the tree tub. Glue the strips of felt and the triangle into a tree shape. Glue the tub into position. Apply rub-down numerals, 1 to 25, to the painted side of the bottle caps and paint with a coat of varnish.
Arrange the caps like Christmas balls on the branches of the felt tree shape and turn a narrow hem on the end of the ribbon. Glue the ribbon onto the felt. Give each ribbon a single twist as it is stuck down so that when the bottle cap is turned to show the picture, the ribbon is lying flat. Insert a glass-headed dressmaker's pin at the top of each ribbon to secure. Snip the ends of the pins off that protrude on the wrong side of the card. Make a ribbon hanger and glue to the top of the card .

## Shoe boxes

**Save cardboard boxes and shoe boxes and put them away for a very rainy day because a strong, well-made box can be turned into one of a variety of fascinating toys.**
**Here are just a few ideas – you'll think up others yourself.**

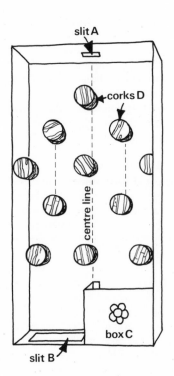

*▲ Glue halves of corks in positions shown*

Cover the box with paper if desired. Make a slit in the centre of the top edge long enough to take a coin. (A)
Cut a larger slit on the bottom edge. This slit must be large enough to allow coins to drop right through and not settle on the edge of the box inside. (B)
Cut the cereal box down by about 1 inch and glue it to the back of the box in the bottom right hand corner. (C)
Glue the corks in the positions shown. You can add more corks if you like but make sure that coins slip through the maze easily. (D)
Tape the lid onto the box if this is the way you want to play the game. Alternatively, cut open a plastic film food bag and tape it over the box

# 78

## Cork bagatelle

This is quite a good game to play with visiting uncles who have a sporting instinct. Play as follows: coins are put in through the slit at the top of the box. If the punter wins, they go through a maze of corks and slip out at the bottom. Unlucky players lose their pennies into the trap inside the box. It's all quite fair and a game of chance.
The bagatelle illustrated has a clear film top, cut from a food bag, so that you can see how to arrange the corks, but the game works just as well and perhaps more excitingly if the lid of the box is taped on so that the player doesn't know whether he is winning or losing until his coin disappears.

Materials you will need:
Shallow box with lid
Gift wrapping paper if desired
Small cereal box or a similar sized box
6 corks cut in half
Adhesive
Sharp knife

# 79

## Shoe box carrycot

A pretty carry cot for a doll complete with a fitted mattress, a matching pillow and a quilted coverlet.

Materials you will need:
Patterned fabric for the outside of the cot
White quilted nylon for the lining
Non-woven interlining fabric for the hood
Roll of cottonwool or piece of wadding
Patterned fabric for the mattress and pillow
Plain fabric for the coverlet
Plastic foam for the mattress and pillow
Fabric adhesive
Paper handkerchiefs

**79.** *Cutting diagram for the carrycot hood and lining sections and the hood made up* ▼

## Mattress and pillow

Cut the plastic foam to fit the bottom of the box. Cut two pieces of the fabric to the same size plus $1\frac{1}{2}$ inches all round. Pin the two pieces together, right sides facing and seam on three sides to make a bag. Insert the foam pad and slip stitch to close the fourth side.

Make a pillow in the same way.

## To make the coverlet

Cut the plain fabric to the size of the box bottom plus 2 inches all round. Cut a piece of cotton wool 1 inch smaller all round. Tack the cotton wool to the wrong side of the fabric.

Place a paper handkerchief on top of the cotton wool and tack it to the fabric. Machine stitch through all thicknesses using a large stitch to quilt the plain fabric. The coverlet illustrated was quilted in squares but diamond patterns or circles would look pretty.

Cut a piece of patterned fabric to the same width as the plain fabric but cut it 3 inches longer. Make a narrow hem on one short end. Place the quilted section on the patterned fabric, right sides facing and the edges of three sides matching. Fold the $2\frac{1}{2}$ inches of patterned fabric back over to the wrong side of the quilting for a turn-down. Pin and tack on both long sides and the other short end. Machine stitch all round these three sides taking a $\frac{1}{2}$ inch seam. Turn the coverlet to the right side and press the turn-down very lightly.

## Making the carrycot

Cut a piece of quilted nylon to fit the bottom of the box, plus $\frac{1}{2}$ inch all round. Measure the box all round the sides and cut a strip of quilting to the total measurement plus 1 inch by the depth of the box plus 1 inch.

Join the strip on the short ends. Seam the bottom piece to one raw edge of the joined strip.

Cut a piece of fabric to cover the outside of the box.

Fold up the fabric at one short end and take it over to the inside of the box. Glue along the raw edge of the inside of the box.

Fold up and glue the other short end in the same way.

Now bring up the long sides, making a fold at the corners, and glue the long sides to the inside of the box.

Turn a narrow hem on the raw edge of the quilted nylon lining and pin it.

## Making up the hood

Cut the hood shape from the diagram, in both outer fabric and lining. Seam A-a-A and B-b-B to shape the hood. When both fabric and lining sections are completed, turn the lining inside out and slip it into the fabric hood. Glue one to the other round the edges.

Put the hood section into position in the box and glue it to the box sides. Insert the quilted nylon lining and glue this to the inside of the box, covering the raw edges of the outside fabric and the raw edges of the hood section. Remove the pins as you work.

Cut a strip of the outer fabric for a strap, 56 inches long and 2 inches wide. Seam the short ends, then fold and machine stitch to make a strap.

The box rests on the doubled strap and is glued to it just below the edge in two places on both sides.

## Other things to make:
### Punch and Judy stand

Cut a square hole in the lid. Make a shelf from the piece cut out. Cut a round hole in the bottom of the box to get an arm through. Cover the box with striped paper or paint it.

### Simple cart

Push a cotton reel onto a long knitting needle and push the needle through one side of the box, near the bottom and out on the other side. Push another cotton reel on the pointed end and stick a small piece of Plasticine on the point to keep the wheel on. Make another pair of wheels and fix them to the box in the same way.

### Rocker bed

Cut rockers from the box lid. Cut sections out of both rockers so that the base of the box fits into them. Glue the rockers on.

### Garage

Simply cut double doors at one end.

# Weaving loom

The loom will make woven fabric up to 5 inches wide and 8 inches long. Join pieces of weaving to make scarves, bags, belts, hats, placemats and, if you feel really ambitious, join pieces to make a garment.

Materials you will need:
Shoe box
Two combs
Stiff card
Knitting yarn of different colours
Two pieces of wood $\frac{1}{4}$ inch by $\frac{1}{4}$ inch, the width of the box
Long darning needle
All-purpose adhesive
Epoxy adhesive
Pair of pliers

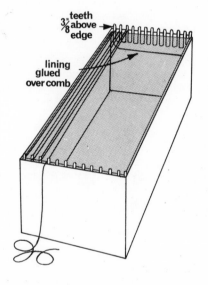

$\frac{3}{8}$" teeth above edge

lining glued over comb

*If only a narrow width of weaving is required, wind warp threads in the middle of the loom* ▲

Remove every other tooth from the two combs. To do this, pull each one sideways, gripping it with a pair of pliers. The box must be strengthened to take the strain that occurs during stringing up for weaving. Cut pieces of card to exactly the dimensions of the box sides and ends. The pieces must fit well enough to push in and stay in position. Cover all four pieces with a patterned paper and cover the bottom of the box with the same paper. Glue the two combs into position so that the teeth show over the edge about $\frac{3}{8}$ inch. Push the lining pieces into the box. Smear epoxy adhesive along the upper edges of the short end pieces. Push these pieces in and up against the combs. Leave to dry.

Cover the outside of the box with a patterned paper.
The loom is now ready for stringing up.

### The principles of weaving
The threads which run the length of the loom are called 'the warp'. The threads which are woven in and out of the warp are called 'the weft'. The warp threads on this loom are wound round and round the length of the box, each thread lying between the teeth of the comb, which holds them straight. It is important that the threads go through spaces immediately in line so count teeth as you thread up.
Wind as many threads round as you need to achieve a width of fabric. Wind an odd number of threads.
Knot the two ends together.
The warp threads need to be really tight for weaving. Push a piece of the wood behind the threads and against the box end. This will make the threads even more taut. If you find that the threads seem to become loose during the weaving through stretching, slip the second piece of wood behind the threads at the other end.

### Weaving on the loom
Thread the needle with the first colour. Weave it under the first warp thread, over the second, under the third and over the fourth and so on to the end. At the end, weave back the other way going over the first thread and under the second.
When you have finished weaving, remove the fabric from the loom by cutting the warp threads with ends about 4 inches long. Darn these ends back into the fabric.

# Shoe box cinema

Cut a viewing hole in the middle of one short end of the box. Cut it about 2 inches wide.
Cut another hole at the other short end. Make this one $3\frac{1}{2}$ inches wide by 3 inches deep. This is for the screen. Line the box with a dark toned paper – black if possible.
From stiff black paper, or some card painted black, cut three rows of heads for the audience. Make each row the exact width of the box but cut one row

$1\frac{1}{2}$ inches deep, the next 2 inches deep and the third $2\frac{1}{2}$ inches deep. Add $\frac{1}{2}$ inch to the depth of each to fold over for the base.
Look through the peephole to judge the distance between each row; the tallest goes at the back and the shortest at the front. Glue the three rows down to the bottom of the box.

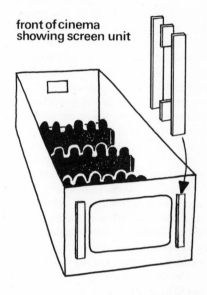

front of cinema showing screen unit

*The shoebox cinema with the lid off and showing the screen construction* ▲

Cover the screen aperture with a piece of plastic film cut from a food bag. Fix it in position on the back of the screen with Sellotape.
Cut four pieces of card $3\frac{1}{2}$ inches deep by $\frac{3}{8}$ inch wide. Glue one at each side of the screen, about $\frac{1}{2}$ inch from the cut edges, on the outside of the box. Cut four pieces of card about $\frac{3}{8}$ inch square. Glue one on each end of the pieces of card already glued to the box. When the strips are dry, glue the remaining $3\frac{1}{2}$ inch long strips in position, putting adhesive on the ends only. This makes a slot for the 'film strip' to slide through. Glue a piece of opaque paper, such as tracing paper, over the back of the screen, glueing it to the strips. Cut it to fit exactly.
Cover the outside of the box with a suitable gift wrapping paper and cut pictures from colour pages of magazines for film advertisements. Glue them to the outside of the box.
Make film strips by cutting up cartoon strips from newspapers and magazines and pasting them into a continuous strip. Pull the strip through the slot.
The box lid goes on during film shows.

# Window sill gardens

Make a window sill garden for a child with flowerpots made from yoghurt and cream pots, cottage cheese tubs and frozen food trays. Paint the pots and cut a hole in the bottom for drainage. Fill the pots with good garden soil or with a proprietary garden compost. All kinds of seeds and pips will grow into fascinating plants on a window sill. Mixed bird seed comes up very quickly and there's always a certain amount of mystery about what all the shoots will grow to be. Orange pips take a long time to germinate and so do grapefruit and lemon pips. Start these off in a dark, warm place, and keep the soil damp. Peas and beans look pretty and come up quickly, and some of the seeds from kitchen jars will produce unusual looking plants. Try cardomom seeds for instance. Avocado stones, apricot and peach kernels grow satisfactorily but they will have to be transferred to a larger pot in about a year.

Small bulbs and corms are fun for a child to grow, such as scillas, crocus, grape hyacinths and snowdrops; and among annuals, pansies, alyssum, lobelia and Virginia stock are about the right scale for flower pot growing. Mustard and cress are quick growers and can be grown on damp blotting paper placed in a frozen food tray. Chinese bean shoots, obtainable from Chinese grocery shops, grow quite quickly to an inch high and can be harvested for supper.

# Fun with nut shells

Nut shells are useful for all kinds of games. Walnuts and hazel nuts can be used to replace counters and the old game of five stones can be played with hazel nuts – they balance on the back of the fingers very well.

Hazel nuts roll well enough to replace marbles in some games and Brazil nuts can be turned into weird looking animals by glueing matchstick legs and scraps of felt to them. (Apricot and peach kernels make animals in the same way too). Walnuts, hazel nuts and peanuts can be threaded onto twine to make peasant-looking necklaces by piercing with a pointed tool.

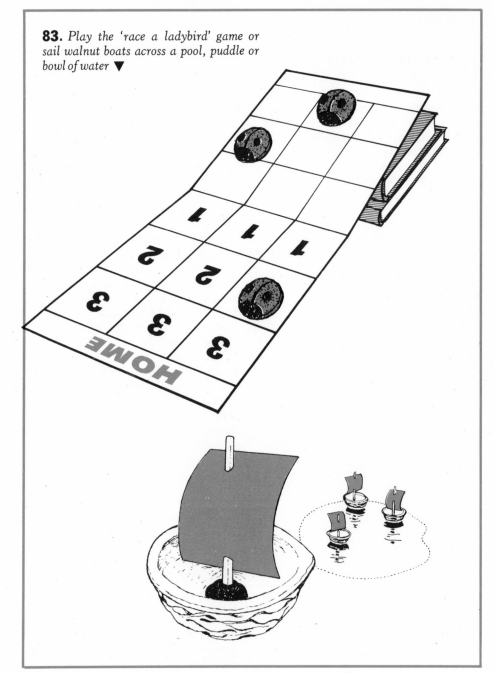

**83.** *Play the 'race a ladybird' game or sail walnut boats across a pool, puddle or bowl of water* ▼

## Ladybirds

Keep only perfect half shells from walnuts. Paint the shells scarlet with black spots and paint a black head on one end.

Put a marble under the ladybird and place the shell on a sloping piece of card or a book and the ladybird will run down the slope very fast. Races can be run with ladybird shells by planning a race-track on a piece of card with 'home' marked at one end.

Walnut shells make very sea-worthy boats too. Cut a small sail from paper and make two vertical slits in it. Push a matchstick through the slits. and glue the matchstick to the bottom of the shell. The matchstick can be stood up in a small piece of Plasticine instead but this makes the boat sink a little lower in the water.

Place a fleet of shells on a bowl of water, lining them up at one side. Blow hard on the sails and the fleet will make for open sea.

On a larger area of water, such as a bathtub, nutshell boats can be raced.

# Building with boxes

Cardboard boxes made of laminated corrugated card are perfect for making toy buildings such as garages, fire stations, police stations, hospitals, etc., The card cuts cleanly, folds well and makes very strong structures.

## Pat's garage

The garage illustrated was made by cutting the top from the box and glueing it to the bottom. This gave the garage two levels, the upper floor reached by a ramp for a car park.
Cut the box as indicated in diagram A. Glue the top portion to the base of the box. Remove the flaps.

Cut openings and doors and make a partial-roof with one of the flaps (diagram B). Cut a hole in the floor of the upper floor and join it to the lower floor with a ramp cut from one of the flaps (diagram C).
These toys need not be painted because corrugated card has a good finish but if decoration is desired, paint with poster paints or enamels.
Standing trees and shrubbery can be cut out of laminated corrugated cardboard and stood around the garage.

## Toys from plastic pots

**All kinds of fascinating toys can be made from plastic food pots – three ideas are given here but more will occur to you once you begin saving them up.**

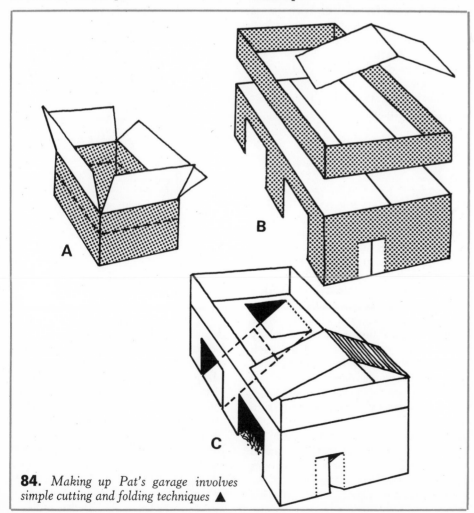

**84.** *Making up Pat's garage involves simple cutting and folding techniques* ▲

## Space men

Little Moonmen – or maybe they are Martians – to make from yoghurt pots or paper coffee cups. Paint each group a different colour to denote their rank in the Space army. Chieftans might be gold with a curtain ring on top, sergeants might be red with double gun muzzles made from cardboard tubes. Plastic straws on top indicate space radio aerials. Exterminate all Earthmen!

## Totem pole

Show children how to decorate food pots to make a fearsome totem pole. Six pots, glued mouth to mouth and base to base make one pole.
Paint the faces with poster paint. Mix a little soap with the paint if it doesn't seem to flow well on the plastic surface. Arms, noses, head-dresses etc., are made from thin cardboard. Slit the pot side with scissors and glue the units into the slits.
Use a good strong adhesive for glueing the pots together.

## Quoits or Ring toss

Once you begin to look around the kitchen, ideas will come to you for using practically everything. The brightly coloured quoits rings illustrated are the outer rims of large plastic tubs, cut off with scissors. The quoit stand is a 12 inch length of $\frac{3}{8}$ inch dowelling sunk into a 4 inch square of $\frac{1}{2}$ inch wood. The stand is topped off with a bead.
The quoits rings are good for hoopla too. Put small objects on a table and toss rings over them to win.

# Punnet work basket

**A pretty work basket for a little girl who loves to sew, made very simply from a plastic fruit punnet.**

Materials you will need:
Plastic punnet
Plastic lid, 3½ inches diameter
36 inch wide fabric, a piece about 12 inches deep
15 inches narrow elastic
1 inch wide white tape
Cotton wool
Piece of cardboard 4½ inches square
Scrap of white ribbon
Felt scraps
Adhesive

▼ *Fish motifs for the basket lid and the needlecase*

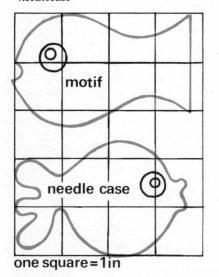

one square = 1 in

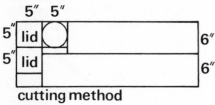

cutting method

▲ *Cut the covering fabric in this way to avoid waste*

Make the padded lid first. Cut two squares of fabric, both 5 inches square. Turn a ¼ inch single hem on all four sides of one piece and press. Mitre the corners neatly. Glue a piece of cotton wool to the centre of the square of card for padding. Place the padded card, cotton wool side up on the wrong side of the second piece of fabric. Turn a ¼ inch hem on all four sides onto the card. Mitre the corners neatly and glue the edges to the card. Cut 4 inches of white ribbon, fold it and glue the two ends together on one of the corners.

Place the square of fabric already prepared on top of the cotton wool, wrong sides facing, then stab stitch both pieces of fabric all round, making the stitches almost invisible, and sewing through the ribbon on the corner.

### Lining the basket

Cut a circle of fabric 5 inches in diameter. Cut the remaining fabric up into 6 inch deep strips and seam them to make a strip approximately 56 inches long. Gather one long edge to fit round the seam line of the fabric circle. Pin and baste the gathered edge to the edge of the circle and then machine stitch. Turn a single ½ inch hem on the remaining long edge and stitch white tape over the raw edge to make an casing for the elastic. (You can, if you prefer, use self fabric for the casing instead of tape). Leave 1 inch open to insert the elastic.
Insert the elastic into the casing and sew the ends. Close the casing.
Slip the lining into the basket and pull the elastic over the basket edge. Arrange the gathers fully on the corners. The elastic will fit under the rim and hold. Cut a fish motif from felt and decorate it with flowerlets cut from a scrap of lace edging. Cut felt eyes and bubbles. Glue the motifs onto the lid.
Make a fish needlecase by cutting out four shapes in felt and machining them together along the straight edge. Cut out and glue on the eyes.

# Ninepins

Almost any kind of plastic container will do to make the ninepins – those containing washing up liquid are good and so are the soft drink bottles.
The ninepins illustrated contained a household cleaning powder.
Give the containers a coat of white emulsion paint first to block out any printed matter on the sides. Paint each container the same, in multicoloured stripes or in a single colour.
Number them from one to nine with a rub down numeral or a number cut from a calendar.
If the ninepins seem to fall over too easily, put a little water, earth, or sand in each one to make them heavier. A rubber ball about 4 inches in diameter is the right scale for playing the ninepins game.

# Standing doll

**A doll with the look of a country lady all dressed up for market day, made from a plastic container and scraps of fabric. The method for making this doll can be applied to dolls to make other characters.**

### Mrs Murphy doll

Materials you will need:
Plastic container (the one used for the doll illustrated contained household salt)
2 sections from an egg carton
White stockinette material (or heavy gauze)
Fabric for dress and jacket
Pink fabric for arms
Knitting yarn for hair
Net and lace for underskirt
Bias binding
Felt
Polyfilla or similar substance
Small beads
Paints
Varnish

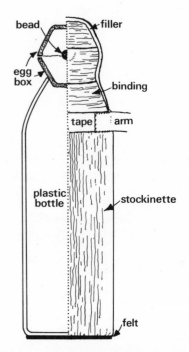

Cover the container with the stockingette material leaving the base uncovered. Make the head by glueing the open ends of two egg box sections together. Bind them round with thin strips of stockingette material to give a smooth, firm finish. Insert a bead for the nose and bind round the whole head again. Sew the head to the top of the bottle. Mould the head and neck with Pollyfilla or similar material. It will probably need two or three layers. When dry paint the

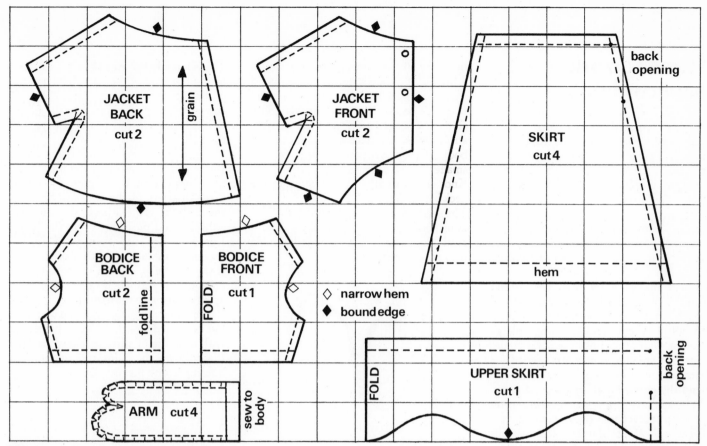

**90.** *Graph pattern for Mrs. Murphy's clothes.* 1 *square*= 1 *inch* ▲

head, face and neck pink. Paint the features.

Varnish the entire surface of the neck and face.

**To make the arms:** Cut the arms from pink fabric. Seam by hand with very small stitches. Clip curves and turn to the right side. Fill with kapok. Sew the arms to the body.

**Hair** Cut the wool into 10 inch lengths and sew to a strip of pink material. Fold back onto itself at either side and catch up all the way round. Glue the material to the head.

### Clothes

**Underskirt** Cut a piece of net approximately 5 inches wide by 20 inches long. Gather the long edge to fit around the waist. Trim with lace edging.

**Dress** Cut bodice pieces from pattern. Join shoulders and underarm seams. Make hem down each side of the bodice at the back. Turn in a small hem round back and armholes. Sew velvet ribbon round the neck. Cut out upper skirt pattern, placing to fold. Join the back seam. Finish lower edge with bias binding. Cut four sections for the main skirt. Join together 3 sections leaving the last one open to match upper skirt. Sew both to the bodice. Turn up ½ inch hem and decorate with lace. Dress doll and join back opening.

**Jacket** Cut the pattern pieces. Join centre back, shoulders and underarm seams. Clip and turn. Finish complete edge with bias binding. Sew on the beads. To finish off the doll, cut a circle of felt to cover the base of the container and glue it on.

# From sea and country

**By building decorations and models from natural things collected on country walks or visits to the sea, children will be encouraged to look for and collect beautiful things themselves.**

**Collage nature pictures made from collections of sea shells, leaves and leaves skeletons, feathers, flower heads, butterfly wings and seeds, arranged and glued to pieces of card, make charming wall decorations with an educational value too.**

## Treasure jars

Arrange a collection of sea shells and stones on the lid of a squat shaped kitchen jar or large preserves jar. Glue the arrangement in place firmly with a waterproof adhesive. Plasticine can be added for colour if you like. Fill the jar with clear water and screw the lid on. Stand the jar on the lid. The water magnifies the display in a most impressive way and makes a very satisfactory way for children to keep their treasures. Display jars make very acceptable gifts for adults and give children an added incentive to choose shells and stones carefully during beach-combing trips.

## Owls on branches

Choose branches of wood with suitable perching places.

Paint pine cones with clear varnish to make them shine and to secure the seeds. Make astonished-looking eyes from black and white paper or scraps of felt. Glue the little owls onto the branches. Fix a picture hook to the back of the branch so that it hangs from a wall.

Alternatively, staple a small curtain ring into the branch and suspend it on invisible nylon thread.

# Stone zoo and paperweights

A single visit to a pebble beach will provide you with enough material to make a whole zoo of animals from beach stones. The four sculptures illustrated are made from stones with only the smallest touch of paint added to enhance the eyes. Otherwise, the stones are exactly as they were found on the beach, with smaller stones grouped round the larger for ears, feet etc. The secret is to look for stones of unusual shape or very smooth stones.

Collect many more than you think you'll need and sit down while at the beach and experiment with stones, grouping them and holding pieces against each other until the ideas come. Then, if smaller stones are needed for ears, feet, tails etc., note the colours and send the children off on a second foray. At home, glue the stones together using a strong contact adhesive or cement.

Paint eyes if absolutely necessary but wherever possible, let the stones themselves suggest the characteristics of the animals.

Glue small stones to large stones where they are needed. Remember to choose some large flat stones for bases.

**To make a paperweight**
Smooth, round stones make ideal paper weights painted with enamel colours.

Either cover the stone's surface with paint completely, applying bold designs or allow the characteristics of the stone to show through the paint. Transfers make an ideal way of decorating stones. Give the transfers a finishing coat of clear varnish.

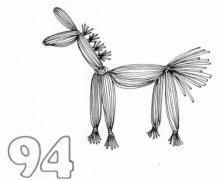

# Grass horses

Make a collection of little green horses from summer grass and let them dry out into hay-coloured horses to keep through the winter months.

Pick several different kinds of grasses, breaking off the stems quite long. Select a bunch of about a dozen stems. Bend the grasses so that the ends are level with the base of the grass heads. Bind along the length using strands of soft, strong grass, to make a head, neck and body. Make two pairs of legs from a smaller bunch of grass.

Knot short lengths of soft grass to the neck for the mane.

The seed heads make a flowing tail.

Alternatively, if long grasses aren't available, make horses from natural raffia using the same method.

# Butterflies from the sea

Mussel shells have the shape of butterfly wings when they are open naturally, but tinted with transparent ink or water colour and suspended from invisible nylon thread, they make a charming butterfly wall hanging and look very realistic.

Choose shells joined in pairs and of different sizes. Drop a little adhesive into the join to make them even more secure.

Thread small glass beads onto fuse wire to make bodies, heads and antennae. If glass beads aren't available, use a short length of gold Christmas gift cord and double it over for body and antennae.

Tie the nylon thread to the shell join and tie the other end to a piece of wood – sea wood if possible.

# Shuttlecock

Shuttlecocks for backyard badminton can be made from a cork and feathers. Use either a large sized cork or the cork cap from a sherry bottle.

The sherry bottle cap usually has holes round the base of the cork. Sharpen the quills of the feathers, dip them in adhesive and push them into the holes. Wind button thread round the base of the quills.

Using a large cork, make holes about $\frac{1}{8}$ inch apart all round the flat top. Wind thin twine round the cork for about three-quarters of the way up. Sharpen the ends of the feathers, dip them in adhesive and push them into the holes. Leave to dry and then wind button thread round the base of the quills.

If the shuttlecock doesn't spin as it flies, open up the feathers by spreading them apart gently with the hand.

Badminton, of course, is played with bats but backyard shuttlecock can be played with a square of stiff cardboard, resting the card on the palm and fingers and holding it with the thumb.

# Kitchen collage

Every day, dozens of things are thrown away with the kitchen rubbish which could be used to make amusing and attractive collages. Take another look at the things around the kitchen and have fun with the shapes. Glued to a piece of paint-sprayed hardboard and framed, everything takes on a different appearance.

This is something children will enjoy doing and you'll probably find their ideas for using things are better than yours!

A few odds and ends you might consider for your first kitchen collage: egg boxes painted in poster colours; beer mats glued flat or at angles; matches and matchboxes, corrugated paper and card cut in strips; paper cups and yoghurt pots glued down by rims and bases; plastic and wooden spoons, milk bottle tops, beer can opening rings, bottle caps, sections cut from plastic squeeze bottles, caps from toothpaste tubes – the possibilities are endless.

Paint the backing board with a matt paint and if the collage units are going to be painted, do this before glueing them down.

Use a good all-purpose adhesive.

Frame with an old picture frame or with strips of 2 inch by $\frac{1}{4}$ inch wood, leaving it unpainted.

# Clothes peg dolls

Clothes pegs are becoming a little more difficult to find but they are still available in some shops and make delightful dolls. The scale of them fits the matchbox furniture.

Cut arms from balsa wood and pierce a hole through the clothes pin just under the knob. The hole can be made by tapping a panel pin through the wood. Pierce a hole in both balsa wood arms. Join them to the body either with hat elastic, tying knots at the 'shoulders' or with black button thread and tying a small bead on the outside of the arm to hold the thread in position.

Paint dolls with poster paints finishing with a coat of clear varnish.

Push the legs of the clothes pins into a blob of Plasticine to make them stand up.

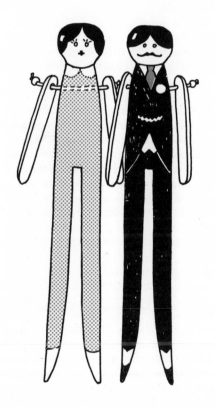

# Matchbox furniture

Start collecting matchboxes and make a whole doll's house full of matchbox furniture for a little girl. Glueing the boxes together into the basic units is quite easy – she could help with this stage. Covering the furniture with coloured paper is slightly more difficult and this has to be done by an adult or an older child.

Three different sizes of matchboxes have been used for the furniture, the giant kitchen size, the ordinary kitchen size and the smoker's size. To make the instructions easier to understand, the giant-sized box is referred to as box A, the ordinary kitchen box as B and the smoker's box as C.

When your grandmother made matchbox furniture she was able to use shoe buttons for drawer knobs so that the matchbox trays pulled out and could be used for storing tiny treasures. A modern alternative that looks almost as good is to sew a small bead through the front of the tray, taking the thread right through the wood and anchoring it to a piece of felt glued to the inside of the tray.

Gift wrapping papers are ideal for covering boxes but choose either a plain colour or a pattern with a small motif to keep the scale looking right.

The cardboard used for the legs, chair-backs etc., is cut from a cereal box.

## Bedroom furniture
**Bed** One large A box with two C boxes glued on as a headboard.

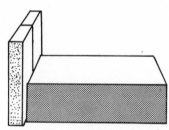

**Dressing table** Two C boxes glued together on their short ends mounted on two groups of two B boxes. The mirror is an ordinary handbag mirror.

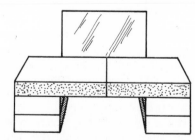

**Dressing table stool** One B matchbox with a supporting leg unit made of cardboard.
**Wardrobe** One A box with four beads for legs.
**Small bureau** Three B boxes and beads for legs.

## Sitting room
**Chesterfield** Eight B boxes, three for the seat, two for arms, three for the back.

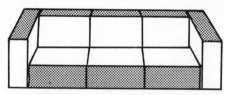

**Armchairs** Two B boxes each with a piece of cardboard holding the angle firm.

**Secretaire** Eight B boxes and a piece of card for the desk top. Four beads for legs.

## Dining room
**Table** Two C boxes mounted on one B box which is then mounted on two B boxes.
**Dining chairs** One B box each with the shell of a second box cut for the chair back and legs.
**Sideboard** Nine B boxes glued together with three of them as drawers.

## Accessories
The television set is one B box with a large flat pearl button glued to it. The box is covered with black paper.

The chesterfield has two small cushions cut from felt and stuffed with cotton wool.

The bed has a pillow made from one motif cut from broderie Anglaise and stitched to a circle of felt.

A lamp is made from a large wooden bead glued to a button with a paper lampshade supported on a matchstick pushed into the bead.

One flower vase is made from a cap from an adhesive tube and the other is a thimble glued to a button and filled with Christmas decorations.

The table mats are cut from scraps of gingham fabric with the edges fringed. The love letter opened on the secretaire is made from paper.

## Covering boxes
Cover the top, sides and bottom of units with one strip of paper wherever possible and keep the join on the underside out of sight. Facing pieces, such as the front of drawers, cupboard doors and the front of the chesterfield are traced off by holding the unit down on the wrong side of the paper and then cutting the shape out very accurately with a sharp blade. If the facing pieces are cut carefully the furniture will have a much better finish.

# Toy town band

Here are some musical instruments to make from odds and ends. Some are easy enough for children to do – others require adult expertise.

**Wrist bells** Make one for each hand – cut 1 inch wide strips of felt and stitch six bells to each band. Close with a press stud or touch and close fastening.

**Tambourine** Glue two paper plates together, rim to rim. Cut four slits in the edge, evenly spaced. Tie narrow ribbon through the slits and tie a bell to each ribbon. A bunch of ribbons tied to the tambourine makes it look very gay.

**Trumpet** Cover the end of a cardboard roll (the kind inside kitchen paper rolls) with a piece of tissue paper. Keep it in place with an elastic band. Make four holes along the cardboard tube with a nail. Make the one nearest the open end a bit larger. Blow through the open end and close the holes with the fingers to make notes.

**Chimes** Cut a piece of wood about 8 inches long. Hang a variety of different sized nails from lengths of twine. Bang the nails with another nail.

**Bottle music** Line up a row of milk bottles or wine bottles. Pour water into them to different levels. The less water the higher the note the bottle will produce. Strike them with a pencil.

**Drum** Choose a round biscuit (cookie) tin if possible, although any shape will do. Cut a piece of parchment big enough to cover the top of the tin and overlap down the sides. Stick Sellotape all round the edge. Make holes all round the edge, just above the tape and thread string through the holes and under the tin to secure the parchment to the mouth of the tin. Drumsticks can be made from leather or suede scraps, stuffed with more scraps and tied to the ends of pieces of dowelling.

**Skiffle bass** For this you need a tea chest but any box made of plywood will do. Screw or bolt a length of broom handle or dowelling to one side in a vertical position. Attach a bass string to the top of the handle and fasten the other end to the centre of the bottom of the chest. Different notes are produced by bending the broom handle slightly away from

the player and slapping at the string.

**Maraccas** Make a pair of papier mâché using an orange as a mould. Glue the two halves together after inserting a few peas or beans. Glue to short lengths of dowelling.

# Canary bird mobile

A pretty, delicate-looking mobile to make from egg shells. The slightest breeze ruffles the feathers and the little birds seem to fly.

Materials you will need:
Shells of six eggs
All purpose adhesive
Soft white paper
Flour and water paste
6 small white beads
3 cocktail sticks
Yellow poster colour
Long needle
White or black button thread
1 yard stiff wire
Plasticine
Black felt-tipped pen

To make the mobile, you need the shells from six eggs. Wash them out and leave to dry. Glue the edges back together again to make complete eggs.
Cover the eggs with tiny scraps of soft tissue paper. Don't stick the entire surface of the paper down, leave the edges unglued. Paste on about three layers. Flour and water paste is best as it dries white.
Leave the eggs to dry out.
Paint the blunt end of the egg and the underbody pale yellow with poster paint.

Paint the back area bright yellow. Cut the points from three wooden cocktail sticks. Make a small hole in the blunt end of the egg and dipping the stick ends in adhesive, push them into the eggs for beaks.
Leave to dry.
Thread a long sharp needle with white button thread. Tie a small white or yellow bead on the end of the thread. Push the needle through the egg shell, through the egg and out the other side. Draw the thread through until the bead is against the body. If the thread goes through from the rear towards the head, the bird will fly upwards. If the thread goes through from under the breast towards the tail, the bird will fly downwards. Straight up from one side to the other and the bird flies straight.
Thread all the eggshell birds onto thread. Draw in two eyes with a black felt-tipped pen just above and each side of the beak.
You will need a handful of soft white feathers. If chicken breast feathers aren't available, unpick the corner of a feather filled pillow and choose the best. Don't forget the sew the pillow up again.
Glue about eight feathers to the body, the quills lying at about the middle of the bird and the rest of the feathers extending beyond the egg-shell body.
Feathers curve either left or right, depending upon which side of the bird they originally came from. Look at the curve of each feather as you use it and place them on the corresponding side of the egg-shell bird.
Hang the birds from their threads to dry.

### Making the mobile
You will need 3 lengths of thin but strong wire, a pair of pliers, black button thread and some small lumps of plasticine. The secret of mobile making is to tie a thread round the exact middle of the first piece of wire and hang this up first. Move the thread until the wire balances. Put the first bird onto one end of the wire, holding the other end. Then put a piece of plasticine on the end to balance the bird while you plan the next unit. As each unit is added, balance the other side of the mobile with lumps of plasticine, removing it as birds are added.
To suspend the birds, cut the thread off to the length you need. Tie a small loop in the end, round a cocktail stick. Slip the loop onto the wire and then drip one drop of clear adhesive onto the loop to secure it to the wire.

INVENTORY 1983